D0103733

Can Christians be genuine peacemakers in our fragmented, polarized world? I hope so, and when I read books like Catherine McNiel's *Fearing Bravely*, I am encouraged. McNiel is a wonderful storyteller, and her wisdom, honesty, and commitment to Jesus and Scripture shepherd us toward becoming better human beings. This practical and engaging book draws us to love God and love our neighbors more deeply, despite the forces that drive wedges between us. I encourage you to read this book with others so you can discern together how you might take risks to love more authentically.

REV. DR. DENNIS R. EDWARDS, associate professor of New Testament, North Park Theological Seminary; author of *Might from the Margins*

At a time when many Christians feel threatened and afraid, Catherine McNiel calls us to courage, inviting us to love our neighbors, strangers, and even enemies in countercultural ways rooted in the example of Jesus. I hope Christians everywhere will read—and heed—this wise, insightful, and challenging book, for the sake of vulnerable neighbors and, even more urgently, to reclaim the public witness of the church.

MATTHEW SOERENS, US director of church mobilization and advocacy, World Relief; coauthor of *Welcoming the Stranger: Justice, Compassion and Truth in the Immigration Debate*

Fear, or fear of God? Whom or what do we fear, and what does that imply for our lives in a world that is not safe? How does our fear of God or fear of someone or something else influence our love for neighbors? This book is powerful, calling us to live the life Jesus intended for us, not a bland and ineffective faith or a vicious nationalistic faith mistaken for Christianity. In reading *Fearing Bravely*, I could not help but exclaim, "Amen!" because it is so spot-on. And I could not help but reel with conviction because of the weighty truth contained within these pages. We Americans need this book. Catherine's thought and writing are profound and eminently applicable to our current situation. It is worthy of attentive reading and contemplation, which should naturally lead to prayerful action.

MARLENA GRAVES, author of *The Way Up Is Down* and *Forty Days on Being a Nine: Enneagram Daily Reflections*

The repeated biblical admonition "Fear not!" strikes many of us as naive and unrealistic. With the many threats we face today, how can God possibly exhort us not to be afraid? The Christian virtues of faith, hope, and love are for long-dead saints living in easier, simpler times in ages past, right? Not so, says Catherine McNiel. In *Fearing Bravely*, she capably demonstrates why we can, in fact, let go of fear and choose instead the risky, cruciform way of love. She does so with the winsomeness of a storyteller, the gentleness of a pastor, and the chutzpah of a prophet. In *Fearing Bravely*, McNiel has given us an invaluable gift: The opportunity to confront and repent of our fear-full malformation as Christians so that we can pursue Jesus' better way of neighbor-, stranger-, and enemy-love. I pray many will take, read, and heed the powerful message of this timely book.

REV. DR. EMILY HUNTER McGOWIN, assistant professor of theology, Wheaton College

Powerful. Convicting. Encouraging. In our broken world today, Catherine McNiel's call to live a life of active love that resists fear rings true and bold. *Fearing Bravely* guides us to confront the things we hate and our greatest fears, from neighbors and strangers to political realities, with the love of Jesus.

> **MICHELLE AMI REYES,** vice president, Asian American Christian Collaborative; author of *Becoming All Things: How Small Changes Lead to Lasting Connections Across Cultures*

This is the book author Catherine McNiel was born to write. Her words are compassionate, prophetic, and for such a time as this. For anyone who wants to love as Jesus loved, especially in the midst of our increasingly divided world, this book is a gentle guide and a tough coach all at once. With theological acumen and a sharp wit, McNiel reminds the church who we are meant to be—a people who love Jesus through the act of loving our neighbors, strangers, and enemies.

> **AUBREY SAMPSON,** church planter and pastor at Renewal Church; speaker; author of *Known*, *The Louder Song*, and *Overcomer*

McNiel has written a biblically sharp and practically wise book that points the way forward for how disciples of Jesus can overcome their fears in order to live lives of hospitality, friendship, and love for neighbors, friends, and family. This book is a perfect text for individuals and church groups hoping to embody the teachings and life of Jesus.

> **JOSHUA W. JIPP,** associate professor of New Testament, Trinity Evangelical Divinity School; author of *Saved by Faith and Hospitality*

Catherine gently shepherds us out of the tunnels of fear and into the meadows of love. Her words are elegant and incisive, but—more importantly—they are generous and kind. I long to offer this book to family and community members who have for too long been guided by suspicion of the Other. It is an invitation to emerge from the trenches and break bread at God's table together.

LIUAN HUSKA, author of *Hurting Yet Whole: Reconciling Body and Spirit in Chronic Pain and Illness*

Catherine has lifted the rug off the elephant in the room of cultural engagement and our changing world. People are afraid—period. They try to dress it up with political, theological, or sociological arguments, but in the end, the core issue is that people are afraid of change and are struggling to hold on to the past. The solution that Catherine offers is not for us to deny the fear but to trust that God is at work, stay on mission, and then let love and justice roll. Be the change!

DR. ALEJANDRO MANDES, executive director of EFCA's All People Initiative; author of *Embracing the New Samaria*

If there's one thing we know our world needs, it is a fresh call for Christians to actively show and share what Jesus is like by the way we love one another and the way we love our neighbors. But as Catherine McNeil shows us in *Fearing Bravely*, we cannot step into neighbor love and great works of justice if we do not address our deep-seated fears. With the gentle voice of a pastor and profoundly insightful engagement with Scripture, McNeil shines lights on how our culture has taught us to be overly fearful of things and people, ignorant about what it is we're truly afraid of, and not nearly fearful (in the sense of reverence) enough. Chapter by chapter, Scripture by Scripture, and story by story, *Fearing Bravely* invites us to look at God, the world, and ourselves with fresh eyes, so we may both be healed by and become ambassadors of God's perfect love, which casts out fear.

BRONWYN LEA, author of *Beyond Awkward Side Hugs*

Catherine is a devoted follower of Jesus who seeks to see heaven on earth. Her commitment to the mission of God is not just theory—it is her lifestyle. *Fearing Bravely: Risking Love for Our Neighbors, Strangers, and Enemies* will encourage you to think and invite you to respond. You will be challenged. You will be inspired. You will be confronted. And it will be worth it. If you want to contribute to what God is already doing in this creation, I recommend you read this book.

HANIBAL RODRIGUEZ, senior pastor of Wheaton Bible Church

FEARING BRAVELY

FEARING BRAVELY

RISKING LOVE FOR OUR NEIGHBORS, STRANGERS + ENEMIES

CATHERINE MCNIEL

A NavPress resource published in alliance
with Tyndale House Publishers

NavPress ◖

NavPress is the publishing ministry of The Navigators, an international Christian organization and leader in personal spiritual development. NavPress is committed to helping people grow spiritually and enjoy lives of meaning and hope through personal and group resources that are biblically rooted, culturally relevant, and highly practical.

For more information, visit NavPress.com.

Fearing Bravely: Risking Love for Our Neighbors, Strangers, and Enemies

Copyright © 2022 by Catherine McNiel. All rights reserved.

A NavPress resource published in alliance with Tyndale House Publishers.

NavPress and the NavPress logo are registered trademarks of NavPress, The Navigators, Colorado Springs, CO. *Tyndale* is registered trademark of Tyndale House Ministries. Absence of ® in connection with marks of NavPress or other parties does not indicate an absence of registration of those marks.

The Team: David Zimmerman, Publisher; Caitlyn Carlson, Acquisitions Editor; Elizabeth Schroll, Copy Editor; Olivia Eldredge, Operations Manager; Lindsey Bergsma, Designer

Author photo by Catherine McNiel, copyright © 2021. All rights reserved.

Cover designed and illustrated by Lindsey Bergsma. All rights reserved.

Published in association with the literary agent Don Gates of The Gates Group, www.the-gates-group.com

Some of the anecdotal illustrations in this book are true to life and are included with the permission of the persons involved. All other illustrations are composites of real situations, and any resemblance to people living or dead is purely coincidental.

For information about special discounts for bulk purchases, please contact Tyndale House Publishers at csresponse@tyndale.com, or call 1-855-277-9400.

ISBN 978-1-64158-326-8

Printed in the United States of America

28	27	26	25	24	23	22
7	6	5	4	3	2	1

For Matthew, my orthopraxy.
And for my neighbors:
May you flourish.

Fear is not a Christian habit of mind.

MARILYNNE ROBINSON

❖

God is love.
Whoever lives in love lives in God,
and God in them. . . .
There is no fear in love.
But perfect love drives out fear . . .
The one who fears is not made perfect in love. . . .
And he has given us this command:
Anyone who loves God
must also love their brother and sister.

1 JOHN 4:16, 18, 21

❖

Let all that you do be done in love.

ST. PAUL

CONTENTS

FOREWORD

I HAVE SPENT MY WRITING LIFE inviting followers of Jesus to see their immigrant neighbors as God sees them, and to love them with a fierce and holy love that won't settle for anything less than justice and flourishing for all. This has been God's call to me, and it's one that I've embraced wholeheartedly. But it has been a difficult call because, though we originate in a God who is love, our default isn't to love our neighbors. That is why I'm so grateful that Catherine wrote *Fearing Bravely: Risking Love for our Neighbors, Strangers, and Enemies*. It's a topic that is always timely, always needed. Always.

I met Catherine through the pages of another book she wrote, *Long Days of Small Things: Motherhood as a Spiritual Discipline*. I'm not a mother, so imagine my surprise at how captivated I was by this book. I was so encouraged and inspired by her insights and perspectives. She gave me a theological framework for my daily life. I only read it because I wanted to give it to a good friend who was struggling through the early days of motherhood, and I *did* give it to her. But I also kept a copy for myself because I learned so much about how to walk with Jesus day by day in the ordinary tasks of my days and how to love the women in my life who are mothers. It strikes me now that even then Catherine was helping me love my neighbors as myself.

Much later, I had the privilege of meeting Catherine and talking with her about my own writing. I learned that she is one who walks closely with God, and she writes out of the overflow of the Spirit in her own life. You will sense it too when you encounter the vulnerability of her writing and the freshness of her ideas on neighbor love. She understands that neighbor love isn't romantic or sentimental—it's a call to love in action, which can be messy and complicated. And just like Jesus' love, it's sacrificial and costly. But it is also worth it because Jesus' command to love our neighbors is freeing—it's a blessing to us to obey him and walk in his ways.

Growing up in the faith, I was often taught that the trajectory of the Scriptures is from being lost to being found, from being enslaved to being free, from being a stranger to being a member of the family of God. I see that trajectory in the Scriptures, but overall, I see what Catherine sees: the trajectory of moving from fear to love. C. S. Lewis once said, "Next to the Blessed Sacrament itself, your neighbour is the holiest object presented to your senses."[1] I believe him. I really do. I know my neighbors are image-bearers of God. But in my experience, the hardest teaching of Jesus by far is the call to love our neighbors as ourselves. It's much easier to hate my neighbor, envy my neighbor, slander my neighbor, and fear my neighbor. It seems that no matter how long we have been following Jesus, we need this teaching, this command to love. We need it daily.

There's no doubt that Jesus commands us to love our neighbors—it is not an option for those who follow him. And yet Catherine writes about neighbor love with so much grace and truth that it feels like an invitation. That's why this book is so important. We live in times that are so polarized—we seem to be moving further and further away from each other. As I write these words, we continue to social distance in the midst of a pandemic, a metaphor for the reality we live day by day. Our fears of one another consume us, but Catherine's gentle invitation is to see our neighbors not through the lens of our fears but through the love of our God. She asks us to consider: *Will I continue to be discipled by fear, or can Jesus' love lead me to another way?*

Truth be told, I wasn't even aware of how much fear informed my interactions with those Jesus has called me to love until Catherine's words asked me to pay attention to my fears and begin to move toward Jesus' love. She will inspire you, too. Find a comfortable, cozy spot; bring your highlighter and a cup of tea; and prepare to be challenged to love extravagantly as you dive into *Fearing Bravely*.

Karen González
author of The God Who Sees: Immigrants, the Bible,
and the Journey to Belong

A NOTE TO THE READER

Dear Reader,

I wrote this book so that together we can learn about, wrestle with, and overcome the fears that get in the way of love. I wrote out of my longing for us to choose to be brave with our fear and courageous with each other.

But conversations about love, fear, neighbors, strangers, and enemies always come from a particular place and perspective. I am a white American citizen, a practicing Christian, and I know that my words and thoughts and stories reflect that particular place and perspective. People from different backgrounds experience the dynamics of power, fear, love, and courage differently. I cannot fully understand or express the dynamics you may face, but I hope that what I've written here will help you arrive at language for your own journey. I come to you with open hands, praying that we can help each other along the way.

Together, may we find the love that overcomes all our fear.

Catherine

DON'T BE AFRAID

Fear is your best friend or your worst enemy. It's like fire.
If you can control it, it can cook for you; it can heat your house.
If you can't control it, it will burn everything
around you and destroy you.

MIKE TYSON,
PARAPHRASING CUS D'AMATO

SUNDAY MORNING, EARLY. The air is cool and moist. It is not yet dawn, but the Sabbath is over and the women have been busy for hours, determined to finish the work left over from Friday night.

That horrible night.

Some tasks must be done, no matter how overpowering the grief. Sometimes the only way to stop from drowning is to keep working.

This is the third day. On Friday, Joseph brought the broken body to the tomb, quickly wrapping it in linen before sundown. The women—who had watched everything—followed to see where he was laid. Now that the Sabbath has ended, they will complete the rites for a dead body. This will be an arduous task, emotionally and physically. They brace themselves as they walk into the tomb.

But the grave is empty. There is nothing there.

The women glance at each other, confused and afraid. When your teacher has been executed, you are never safe. Not anywhere, but especially not here. *Who has taken the body? Is this a trap?*

Then, two men suddenly appear before them. Shocking enough in this dark, secluded place, but worse, these men shine like lightning. The women can hardly look at the brightness. Trembling, they grip each other, shielding their eyes, trying not to collapse in fear.

The men begin to speak, words the women cannot absorb, words that cannot be true. Words that will change everything. The lightning men look these women in the eyes and say:

Why do you look for the living among the dead? He
is not here; he has risen! Remember how he told you,
while he was still with you?[1]

And then they do remember.

The women sink against the cave stones in shock, hearts
pounding, minds spinning. Could it be true? Then they stand,
they run. They run to tell their friends, the hiding, terrified,
devastated followers of Jesus. These women have been entrusted
with the most unbelievable message, and they will tell it. The
world will know.

———————

Sunday night, late. A group of friends huddle, terrified, inside
the upper room of a house, the doors locked. Can you blame
them? Days ago, their friend and teacher was brutally and publicly executed. No wonder they hide.

They live in an oppressed nation under the thumb of a violent empire. They could have laid low, but no—they stepped
out to follow a man who ended up provoking the authorities
with the treasonous, blasphemous claim that he was both King
and God. He was crucified for that claim. Just days ago they
were celebrating Passover together, remembering God's salvation, their ancestors' liberation from another violent empire.
Today, they shelter in place. The doors are locked. The world is
too dangerous for them now.

But then, in that shut-up room, Jesus appears.

Jesus is right there. He doesn't knock on the door, doesn't

jiggle the handle. The door was locked, the disciples were inside, and Jesus was dead—but then he is there, standing before them. He is in the room with them, saying, "Peace be with you. Don't be afraid."

As they stand with their hearts pounding, he asks them, "Do you have anything here to eat?"[2]

A snack. He asks for a snack.

These stunned and terrified friends are overjoyed.

The empire is still violent. Their teacher is still an enemy of the state. Powerful people remain hell-bent on silencing those who teach that God's Kingdom rests on mercy and justice, not greed and oppression. The dangers do not evaporate with Jesus' resurrection—they multiply. This community will huddle in this room many times in the months to come, sheltering, praying. They will never be safe or successful by any normal definition. Life will never be "normal" again, not ever, not at all.

Only one thing has changed, and somehow, that one thing is enough to change everything:

Jesus is in the room.

CHAPTER I

WHOM SHALL I FEAR?

I SAT IN THE BACK OF THE CHURCH SANCTUARY on a muggy summer evening, head in my hands. Worship music filled the room, and flies buzzed around noisy ceiling fans, but I could hear God's gentle voice as clearly as if Jesus were sitting beside me in the pew:

It's time. Time to put aside your fear. It's time to learn how to forgive, how to risk, how to love.

But I couldn't. Or rather, I wouldn't. I didn't want to. Old wounds become part of who you are. Old fears die hard.

Back up a step, then, and I'll help you move from there, God prompted. *This is what you need to do. Life is better on the other side.*

Silence from me.

The music played on. Flies landed on my shoulders. Pews groaned in the heat.

Then: *Do you want to want to forgive?*

No. No. I didn't even want to want to forgive.

The trauma I experienced was a decade old by then, but the pain stayed fresh. The people who harmed me had not asked for my forgiveness, and I did not offer it. Over time, wounds reshaped themselves into fear—a protective reflex against future pain. Mistrust became the lens through which I viewed everyone.

I spent years wrestling against being known. Healing requires healthy relationships and caring community, but fear had such a solid head start. I hadn't consciously put walls up to protect myself, but the barriers were there all the same, tall and strong. I'd grown skilled at keeping would-be friends from getting close enough to hurt me—or love me—lest they tear open old wounds. But the walls I'd built to protect myself merely trapped me alone with fear.

In a vicious cycle, fear kept me from the love I needed to escape fear.

I'd reached a crisis point, a fork in the road. God asked me to move forward, toward a love that casts out fear. Fear fought to retain control, keeping me from love. Which would I choose? I could not try to serve them both.

God sat beside me in that humid room for a long, long time, gently backing me up step-by-step until we arrived at a starting place so miniscule I agreed to try.

———

Most of us reach that fork in the road at some point. We've been harmed by others, and our pain and distrust informs how we proceed through life, how we view those around us. But rather than leading us to safety, fear holds us in chains. Only in risking love will we find freedom.

But to do that, we must be honest with ourselves and name the things we fear, the things that hold us back.

What are some of these things for you?

I'm not talking about feeling anxious or insecure, like finding a spider on your jeans, or feeling nervous at parties. I'm talking about fears that are deeper, more fundamental, fears that shape our relationships and communities and cultures. Like the dread of life becoming unstable, the devastating aftermath of trauma, or the precariousness of loving in a world that offers no guarantees.

These deeper fears don't just live in our heads and hearts; they have direct repercussions on other human beings. They nudge us to view people as inherently worthy of our distrust or contempt, rather than fellow humans we are called to love. I hear these messages expressed out loud almost every day. They take up so much bandwidth in our collective consciousness that we may not realize the words and implications are rooted in fear. After all, fear sounds like weakness, and these warnings seem so right and wise.

But sometimes what sounds like wisdom is in tension with God's good news.

Jesus commands us to love our neighbors. But we often hold our neighbors at arm's length.

God instructs us to welcome strangers, never withholding hospitality or help from anyone in need. But we have a tendency to fear strangers, especially those needing hospitality, afraid that their presence and neediness may threaten what we have.

Jesus taught us to love our enemies and pray for those who actively harm us. But this goes against every instinct we have. Sometimes we even create enemies, for it's so easy to see anyone who thinks, believes, looks, or lives differently from us as dangerous, a threat to our way of life.

God calls us to set aside our rights in order to seek justice for the most vulnerable. But our culture—through the news, television, social media, and even pulpits—suggests it would be safer to limit the rights of others lest our own rights be threatened.

The Bible warns us not to be overcome by evil, but to overcome evil with good. Yet how often do we allow our fear of evil to overcome the goodness in ourselves and others?

The resurrected Son of God told his friends to be at peace during times of trouble, because his love would remain with them always. But if my own heart is any gauge, we often suspect there is not nearly enough love to go around.

In countless little ways, fear wins us over every day.

FEAR, OUR FRENEMY

But let's back up for a second and consider how we got here. After all, fear isn't always an enemy.

This world is full of dangers, and fear is a necessary part of our basic survival package. Without fear, life would be a nightmare, and a short one. My toddlers leapt into deep swimming pools, chased squirrels onto busy streets, and tried to hurl themselves (and anything they could lift) out of our third-story apartment window. After a few exhausting years keeping them alive and intact, I praised God for their ability to feel afraid.

Eventually the hot stove, the terrifying moment searching for mom and dad in the crowd, and the shock at the electric outlet compelled my children to accumulate survival skills and common sense. Their pain receptors triggered a fear response in the amygdala and altered their permanent record. They make better choices now.

The amygdala is a tiny organ sitting just above the brain stem, that precious area of our bodies regulating heartbeat and breath. The amygdala's job is to accumulate data from our senses and provide rapid chemical reactions, responding swiftly and decisively to threats before our conscious minds even register what's happening. The amygdala prepares us for fight or flight, whether we want to or not. I'm grateful; without the amygdala, few of us would see adulthood.[1]

So actually, fear is a friend. Fear allows us to learn and grow, motivates us to create and innovate. Fear opens the doors to life and love, safety and survival.

But our friend fear can become a frenemy, as they say, because we are never unbiased observers of reality. Our brains don't merely read the world; they interpret the world, creating a feedback loop.[2] Our assumptions influence what we see— and, as the old proverb says, when your only tool is a hammer, everything you see looks like a nail. With our brain wired and ready for fear, we start seeing a world full of threats, including many that do not exist. This false perception shapes how we live and behave and approach others, until it returns us full circle: Through self-fulfilling prophecy, we create the dangers we most fear.

And fear is contagious. Society is structured to manipulate

and multiply our fears to feed its own lusts. Ancient kings and priests exploited fears and vulnerabilities to keep their people passive and obedient. Today's influencers—more corporate than kingly—are just as eager for wealth and power. They, too, have perfected fear as a tool to exploit our triggers, sending us more and more terrifying data, training us to return to their broadcast, website, political party, or product again and again. We're far more likely to keep the television on if we've been warned that severe weather (or bad news of any sort) is on the way.

Unfortunately, we're not wired for moderation in the fear department. We binge on fear long after the necessity has passed, trapping ourselves in an imaginary world—or a genuinely dangerous world our fears helped create. A steady diet of fear warps its intended purpose. No longer a prompt toward safety and security, fear becomes our destination, an addiction, a pandemic.

Then, when fear goes haywire, it leads to hate. Hate and fear grow deep roots, as generations produce and reproduce conflict and war, vendettas, more hate, more violence, and more fear. This toxic form of fear is invasive. Once it takes root, it takes over. It isolates and divides. We grow comfortable hating our enemies and view strangers suspiciously (after all, they might be enemies). Our own neighbors become strangers to us. We grow obsessed with seeing danger in each other—whether the "other" lives across the street, across the border, or across the globe.

Fear runs rampant in our society; it's become more a habit than a gauge of safety. People in far more dangerous communities around the world live less entrenched in fear than we do. When a recent international survey asked people about their fears, Americans scored significantly higher than the global average. We even outperformed ourselves, presenting more worry, stress, and anger than in years past, our fears increasing even as our economy and health improved.[3] Large majorities of Americans reported an ongoing experience of being "very afraid" and produced a long list of reasons why: government, pollution, finances, illness, death, terrorists, violence, extremists.[4]

These fears are not necessarily unsubstantiated. A glimpse at history (or the newspaper, or Facebook) is enough to demonstrate the countless ways we humans hurt and abuse each other. But how many of those threats were created by people who were afraid? The evil we fear and the evil we create *because of* our fear run together like watercolors until we can't tell them apart.

The next step *should* be our fears energizing us to make changes, build relationships, make the world safer for everyone. But we already know what happens instead. Our families, neighborhoods, churches, and countries build walls, buy weapons, check locks, batten the hatches—and splinter. We've all seen loved ones turn on each other over issues related to politics, the COVID pandemic, social-justice issues. Everyone knows who and what we stand against, who is in and who is out. Paralyzed by worry and dread, we lose our ability to understand each other, to connect, to heal, to build. As our fear turns to hate we resort to violence or neglect; we don't go out of our way to offer compassion to the people we're afraid might destroy our way of life. Since we view ourselves as fighting on the right side, we view this destructive behavior as moral, even altruistic, rather than the evil it is.

As I look into my heart, my neighborhood, my social-media

feeds, and my relationships, I see the abundant harvest decades of living in fear has produced in our society. A self-fulfilling prophecy of fear-that-becomes-hate is at work in our lives and communities. Just five minutes of listening to cable news or reading internet comments should prove my point. The cycle goes on and on, and each one of us is caught up in it to some degree.

Every person on earth, every day, is being molded into a certain shape, taught a particular way of being in the world. Christians call this discipleship, and we have made an intentional choice to be discipled and formed by Jesus and the Spirit. Our lives are meant to center around loving God and our neighbors, worshiping in the presence of God, and producing the fruit of the Spirit together in community.

And yet, so many of the influences we allow to form us are at cross-purposes with this goal. We are committed to choosing love, but we've given fear such a solid head start.

When I type "Christians are" into my search engine, the top hits are not about our love and care for our communities. Rather, many American Christians are known for fear*ful*ness— a fear quickly disintegrating into hatred. For instance, poll after poll suggests that white American evangelicals like myself are twice as likely to believe our safety is threatened by those around us; far more likely to claim long-debunked hoaxes as truth; and out of all Americans, most likely to be viewed by our neighbors as hateful.[5]

Friend, these perceptions weigh on me. Whatever contrasting evidence we might produce, we Christians are not primarily associated with loving others but with being afraid of others.

The *most* afraid, most easily swayed by conspiracy theories, most quickly driven to hatred.

This is a major blow. The Christian community exists to declare and demonstrate God's love, even in difficult, dangerous circumstances. But instead, it seems many of us have been nurtured through fear into hatred, and from hatred to neglect. If God's true people are known by their love as Jesus claimed,[6] we must ask ourselves if God's true people are standing somewhere other than under the sign marked "Christian."

I think back to that night I wrestled my habit of fear against the healing I could find in love. It wasn't that the trauma done to me wasn't real—it was terrible, with lasting impact. The question God put to me was this: Would I continue to be discipled by fear, or could Jesus' love lead me to another way?

THE MOST EXCELLENT WAY

Thousands of years ago, in a culture of factions and oppression and very real reasons to be afraid, Jesus climbed a mountain, sat down, and began to teach the gathered crowd that different path, that narrow road. He taught his followers to love without fear or constraint. Love God with your entire being. Love and care for your neighbor. Love and provide for the stranger. Love and pray for your enemies. Jesus did not merely give lip service to this teaching: he lived it with his body, even when it led to his death.

Years later, the apostle John wrote, "There is no fear in love. But perfect love drives out fear. . . . The one who fears is not made perfect in love."[7] This was not a new idea. We've known for millennia that love is the force strong enough to uproot both fear and its offspring, hate. Connecting to other humans physically, emotionally, and relationally allows our fears to subside on a spiritual as well as chemical and neurological level, a fact that has been confirmed by both ancient wisdom and modern science.[8] This active love is not an easy, breezy feeling, but a lifestyle we must choose daily. Practiced in community, love overturns all these social, generational, neurobiological cycles.

In love, Jesus led the way to unsafe places and situations, confronting injustice and powerful empires, healing people with diseases, eating with sinners, hanging with the marginalized. Jesus wasn't safe—he was publicly executed. Living a life of active love that resists fear and hate is subversive and dangerous. Earthly powers—whether kings, corporations, or cable television—prefer not to be threatened. Yet the night before his detention and crucifixion, Jesus declared that love and unity would mark his followers. Love, even in the face of unsafety and death, is the path of life.

Let me put it bluntly: Fear is not a Christian practice. A society oriented around politicians, the economy, or the media may choose to live in fear, but Christians have already died to themselves and been raised in Christ. What do we have left to lose? Christians are committed to practicing an active love that pours itself out, following Jesus by laying down our rights and even our lives for our friends and neighbors. Even for strangers. Even our enemies. That doesn't leave many people on the planet we are free to abandon. And this practice is not an optional element of faith, either; active love is the center, the thing itself.

This is why practicing faith in community matters so greatly. We cannot tackle this mission on our own.

A few years after Jesus' resurrection, as the early church explored their new identity and the practices of living in community, the apostle Paul wrote a letter to encourage the new Christians in the way of Jesus.[9] *And now I will show you the most excellent way:*

Love is patient, love is kind. We are all broken; how can we rebuild together?

Love does not envy. We are invited to live out of gratitude and contentment, trusting God to provide, sharing openly, not grasping what we have or want, not fearing those who might limit our material comfort.

Love does not boast, it is not proud. We find strength in our weakness, practicing humility. We do not point fingers at "those sinful people" or repel others with our self-righteousness. We lean in, loving, with nothing to prove and nothing to lose.

Love does not dishonor others. We honor every person, even those we were previously trained to fear, even those we were taught held little value: refugees at the border, immigrants in our neighborhoods, people from other backgrounds or ethnicities, those with special needs, the elderly, the infant.

Love is not self-seeking. Holding on to what is ours is not a primary concern. We pour ourselves out.

Love is not easily angered, keeps no record of wrongs. The enemy cycle is broken, for we seek redemption and restoration, not revenge.

Love does not delight in evil but rejoices with the truth. We turn away from news that paints those who are different from us in a negative or suspicious light. We listen for truth, even if truth makes us uncomfortable and challenges our sense of self-righteousness.

Love always protects, always trusts, always hopes, always perseveres. We let go of our lives to find abundant life. We move forward together, with God's Spirit to strengthen and console us.

Love never fails. But where there are prophecies, they will cease; where there are tongues, they will be stilled; where there is knowledge, it will pass away. We do not listen to teachers who preach right doctrine if they do not live out active love. We amplify voices that embody both truth and dignity.

If I speak with the tongue of men and of angels but have not love, I am nothing. Even if I know all the right doctrines, if I have not love, *I am nothing.*

And now these three remain: faith, hope and love. But the greatest of these is love.

AS MUCH AS YOU CAN

I want to ask you to pause for a moment and take a breath. Reach out your hands and heart to God. This is not a small thing we are stepping into, not an easy thing to face. Our fears and concerns are legitimate and heavy; our lives and loved ones are precious.

But there's another layer too: When we hear that God wants us to do something, another set of fears are triggered. What if we fall short? These words of Jesus', well—they do not sound like an invitation, an opportunity to build something beautiful. They sound like a pass/fail exam with the deck stacked against us.

I want to assure you right off the bat that the road we're taking is not paved with legalism, demands so high we can't help but fail. God is not peering over our shoulders, waiting for us to fall. There is grace all the way down.

God's message to us—and the message of this book—is *do not fear*. God invites us to a perfect love. We have no reason to be afraid of failure or rejection. We are empowered by love—unearned, eternal, unfailing love. God's *kindness*, not his hostility, brings us to repentance. This is God's joyful idea, God's jubilant project. This is God's love from beginning to end.

And now, God sets a question before us. We have been made alive and set free by the love of God. *Will we follow Jesus?* Jesus himself warned us to count the cost, for the road is narrow and hard.[10] Few will choose to pick up their cross. But I am writing this, and you are reading it, for we are doing just that: considering this path, counting this cost. After all, no one begins an enormous project without first calculating what it requires.

Part of this calculation is deciding to confront our fears and step out in love, even when it feels terrifying to do so. It means we fear *bravely*, changing our posture toward God's beloved children, whether they be neighbors, strangers, or enemies. This is hard, especially if we aren't accustomed to being asked to follow Jesus with our bodies and lives in addition to believing with our minds. Plus, we cannot complete this mission by ourselves. So, God calls us together into a team, a body, each doing our own small part. We are not saviors. We will destroy ourselves—and each other—if we act like we are. We are hands and feet, working together to make this small change that changes everything.

There is an ancient book called *The Didache*, which means *The Teaching*, considered to be a handbook of the earliest Christians. It ends pages of instructions and commands with these words:

> See that you do not neglect the commandments of the Lord, but keep them just as you received them . . .
> Take care that nobody tempts you away from the path of this Teaching . . . If you can shoulder the Lord's yoke in its entirety, then you will be perfect; but if that is too much for you, do as much as you can.[11]

Do as much as you can. Don't allow fear to tell you the choices are *be perfect* or *never begin*. *Do as much as you can.*

Take a deep breath, friend. You are loved with an everlasting love. When you're ready, come along with me, and centuries of Christ followers before us. Let us go and find the Lord.

CHAPTER 2

UNSAFE AND UNAFRAID

MY HUSBAND LOVES A GOOD AFTERNOON NAP. On Sundays, I often find myself backing quietly out of our bedroom as he mumbles "wake me up in thirty minutes." Half an hour later, I don't tiptoe back in—I make as much noise as possible. He goes from dead asleep to standing up straight in no more than one second. Somehow his subconscious tells him it is time to defend the family from intruders, and, grateful as I am for this instinct, I prefer to be well out of the way.

Once the initial shock is over, he sinks back into the bed to awaken more slowly while I nervously chuckle and mumble something soothing like "everything's fine."

Most of the time we assure our startled loved ones that they needn't be afraid because *nothing is wrong*. Their amygdala are set to misfire, and they need a reorientation: "You're safe at home," "It was just a bad dream," "You let your imagination get the better of you." Like people first arriving in *The Good Place*, we emphasize the stability of their environment: *Everything is fine.*

Sometimes, though, everything is not fine. Sometimes the moment of shock is followed by hardship and pain. When I was a kid, my parents slept with a (rotary landline) phone next to their bed, the ringer always turned on. My dad was the pastor; it wasn't uncommon for him and my mom to be needed in the middle of the night. Tragedy often announces itself with a late-night phone call.

Have you ever been pulled from deep sleep by the dreaded ring of a telephone? There's a sacred heaviness in the darkness during the second or two after you're jolted awake but before you've heard the news. You know life is about to change—but for one last breath, you're still on this side of normal.

Imagine, then, if in that fear-filled moment, the words you heard went against every impulse you felt. Imagine hearing, "Don't be afraid."

Depending on what phrasing and translation you use, there are at least seventy (and as many as several hundred) instances in the Bible when God or his messengers show up and instruct someone not to be afraid. Often the phrase takes a negating syllable and places it next to the word *fear*. In other words, "unfear" or "not-fear." Or, like the King James I grew up reciting at Christmas, "Fear not!" Grammatically, these statements are not suggestions or options but commands. God is not saying, "Try a positive mind-set!" or "Cheer up! Everything is fine!" No, these words, directed to suffering people in dire straits, are imperatives, much-needed directions: "Here's what you should do next: *Not* fear."

The thing is, God often shows up to comfort people who have received a great shock and some bad news. They are not in a safe place. They have ample reason to fear.

A pregnant slave woman runs into the desert away from her owners and abusers. An old man staggers, hearing that his long-dead son may be alive. A community of slaves pack up their children and *go*, their captors in hot pursuit. Countryfolk see an empire's army approaching and send their children into hiding—only to be violently carried away into exile. A young unmarried woman discovers she is pregnant, chosen to carry, birth, and raise the Messiah, the son of God. Friends watch their teacher and friend brutally and publicly murdered before their eyes, knowing their own lives are now on the line. An ever-growing community of social outcasts face persecution, prison, and death if they continue faithfully with their new family and Lord.

It was to these people—and so many more over the centuries—that God said, "Don't be afraid." None of them were safe. Not one. These were not the protected, privileged, and powerful people on top of the world: In most cases, they were simply trying to survive. They had every reason to fear.

And into this unsafe world, God did not say, "Everything will be fine. Don't worry; be happy!" God's message was more like this: "Beloved, I have seen your pain and suffering; don't think for a moment that you've been alone. You've had to do terrible things, and I am asking you to go to places and make choices that will be harder yet. But I am with you."

UNSAFE

We're staring down an uncomfortable question right now: If the world is unsafe *and* God consistently tells his people "do not fear" . . . is God out of his mind? Why would a pregnant young woman recently abandoned *fear not*? Why should a nation of immigrants following nothing but a cloud through the wilderness continue *unafraid*? What would cause a family to face ongoing danger and estrangement *without fear*?

Sometimes God answered these questions, reminding the terrified listener that "I am with you" and proclaiming the strength and certainty of his faithfulness. But the fact remains: These people were not safe. We may not be safe either, particularly if we choose to follow Jesus. But Jesus invites us to realize that safety isn't what matters anymore.

Jesus would have been safe, had he stayed put at God's right hand—but he took on flesh and came to earth. Jesus could have lived under the radar, wandering rural villages and hill country, healing and teaching the farmers and fishermen who loved him—but he traveled to Jerusalem, where all eyes would be on him. Even then Jesus could have stayed away from the temple, from the corrupt religious, political, and economic leaders—or at least laid low and avoided confrontation. Instead, Jesus went where people needed mercy and compassion and relief from injustice; he went straight to those leaders, overturning tables and hierarchies with every turn of phrase. Jesus hung out with lepers and tax collectors and "women of ill repute." He rained down *Woes* upon oppressive landlords and extorting clergy and the patrons from whom he ought to have been currying favor. He cried out for oppressive systems to be overturned, and he used his body as a tool of subversion, healing and loving the wrong people on the wrong day, at the wrong place, in the wrong way. He lived out of love rather than fear, and this meant laying his own life down.

Jesus habitually went to unsafe places and dangerous people and did risky things; he called his followers to do the same. But Jesus didn't cover them (or himself) with a magic spell of protection. Jesus' friends saw him arrested and crucified, a punishment meant to be publicly gruesome, as slow, painful, and graphic a death as possible. Crucifixion was reserved for slaves and enemies of the state, a powerful deterrent to others who might be tempted toward similar behavior.[1] I can imagine that, in their grief, Jesus' friends heard his warning echo in their ears: "If any of you wants to be my follower, you must give up your own way, take up your cross daily, and follow me."[2] These words were never metaphorical to this community long-since stripped of civil rights, forced to watch their neighbors publicly executed along busy highways.[3] We hang crosses around our necks these days, as a symbol of love and beauty. But for Jesus' friends and countrymen, the cross was a well-known symbol of terror, a reminder of their powerlessness before the empire.

If our government were in the habit of watching my internet history for antiestablishment commentary *and* regularly crucifying my fellow countrymen in a show of public warning along I-80, I would be very careful what I said and who I followed— and very, very afraid. That is, after all, how earthly empires wield their power: through fear.

But Jesus' teachings were never instructions on how to fight or flee. He didn't encourage running and hiding *or* gathering power and privilege to protect oneself. Jesus did not imagine our goal would be safety. God, walking the earth, exhorted his friends and students to *engage*, to give sacrificially, to confront the powerful leaders and work toward justice and righteousness. He preached this and he practiced it. And through it all, Jesus taught his friends not to fear but to overcome with love: Love your neighbor, love the stranger, love even your enemy.

Let me not sugarcoat it: This way of living killed him. It put his followers at odds with the political and religious powers of the day. But Jesus told his friends to continue these Kingdom-acts of mercy and justice in his absence, going to unsafe places and risky people, showing compassion to those on the outs and confronting those with power. Even if it killed them too.

And he instructed his followers: "Don't be afraid."

BOMBSHELL

But here's the thing: Jesus' followers *were* afraid. They were notoriously fearful, competitive, and argumentative. Their anxieties shine through as they trip over each other to be first, talk over one another to put their ideas forward, fight over who was the greatest, and (my personal favorite) send their mothers to put in a good word. "Do you not understand how this is going to play out?" Jesus asked, incredulous, his raised eyebrows betraying the degree of their error. "You want to be by my side when this goes down?"[4] Sure enough, when push came to shove, they were terrified. Some turned to fight, others to flight. They fell asleep when he asked them to pray, didn't know how to help when he suffered, couldn't see the outline of a plan in the chaos. Peter denied he knew Jesus at all.

I'm not pointing any fingers here. My amygdala is finely tuned and ready to fire. I don't imagine I'd have left my bread rising in the kitchen to follow Jesus into Jerusalem, and I don't make a habit of cozying up to people about to be publicly executed. But the lesson stands here before us, a stumbling block to me and you and any who would take the name of Jesus: the bar Jesus set for his followers was high. Very high. Too high for most of his closest friends, and too high for me.

And yet, if we are going to use the word *Christian* to describe ourselves, we must at least consider what Jesus asked of his followers. Jesus described a narrow path and a narrow gate and told us to count the cost carefully; if we decide to move forward, we do so carrying a cross.

I get why Jesus' disciples were confused and afraid, even after everything they had seen and heard and done. Nothing about that shocks me. But there's more to this story.

They didn't stay afraid. Something happened that changed everything. After Jesus' resurrection and ascension, the disciples went from fearful and bewildered to utterly bold and joyful. After the living Jesus appeared to them, after he fed them with his own hands and sent them off to build the Kingdom and make disciples, after Jesus poured his Spirit upon them, these fearful fishermen and tax collectors started traveling the world, preaching to the powerful, facing death, loss, and persecution head on—and rejoicing.

What changed? How did they transform from men who lied, ran, fought, and hid behind locked doors—into confident, joyful members of a community, willing to proclaim what they believed was good news, even though it was likely to alienate them, land them in jail, and put them on death row? What did they encounter in the risen Lord, and how can we catch it ourselves?

The teachings of Jesus alone hadn't done it. The disciples had been marinating in the truth of God's Kingdom—first through the Jewish synagogue, then with Jesus, their Rabbi—all their lives. It wasn't even Jesus' presence, for while he was with them, side by side, day after day, they remained hopeful but afraid. Something else made the difference. Something else "transformed a dozen or so disconsolate followers of a slain and discredited leader into one of the most dynamic forces in human history."[5]

The early church made a huge splash. They went throughout the known world, preaching and practicing the way of God's Kingdom, often in direct contradiction to the laws of the empire. They loved and cared not only for their own vulnerable but for strangers and enemies too. The Roman Emperor Julian wrote a letter complaining that his own countrymen (whom he considered morally superior to both Jews and Christians) were causing him to lose credibility:

> Observe how the kindness of Christians to strangers, their care for the burial of their dead, and the sobriety of their lifestyle has done the most to advance their cause[.] Each of these things, I think, ought really to be practiced by us. . . . [T]he impious Galileans support not only their own poor but ours as well.[6]

The people who recalibrated their lives around following Jesus were known for love and compassion, even toward those who were hostile to their existence. In the face of danger, they were fearless in love and joyful in sacrifice. Jesus' parting hope for this community—that though hurting they would find unshakable joy, though scattered they would know the sustaining presence of God, and though plagued with troubles they would know peace—was coming to fruition.[7]

This group of early Christians was never *safe* or *powerful*; their motivation, their passion, and their love was energized by something else entirely.

My question is: What did Jesus and his followers know that we have forgotten?

DISTRACTED BY DOXOLOGY

The Christians in Ephesus also had every reason to be anxious and afraid. They were living in a city layered with religious, political, and economic power. Artemis' religious cult made its home in Ephesus, her temple considered one of the Seven Wonders of the Ancient World. Politically, Ephesus experienced all the seismic disruptions of shifting empires. The Egyptian king Ptolemy XII escaped there, claiming sanctuary in the temple of Artemis. Mark Antony and Cleopatra spent time there. Caesar Augustus himself declared Ephesus a major seat of government and commerce for the Roman Empire.

Imagine being part of the newborn body of Christ in such a place! These people lived out of step with Roman society, living for the Kingdom rather than the empire—and they suffered for it. They lived among forceful authorities, capable of upending their lives and families. They followed a man whose life *had been* ended by the empire in just that way.

But that was the difference. They believed King Jesus could do so much more, that no power exists on earth or in heaven that is not under the feet of Jesus.

That's why the apostle Paul, writing under house arrest,[8] doesn't mention any of these superpowers in his theology-rich letter to the Ephesians. Paul speaks of only one power: that which "raised Christ from the dead and seated him at [God's] right hand in the heavenly realms, far above all rule and authority, power and dominion, and every name that is invoked, not only in the present age but also in the one to come."[9]

What gets me every time in Paul's letter is not only the incredible theology but his writing voice. This man is in prison—but his enthusiasm for the good news of God's Kingdom keeps bursting out, overflowing.

What must it have been like, listening to him speak in person? I imagine him shuffling papers, clearing his throat, starting out calm and clear, logical and linear—but quickly growing distracted by his own excitement, caught up in a fast run-on sentence about the incredible, mysterious truth of God's love and power—made real and full in us! in Christ!—until he's waving his arms around and shouting in full-blown doxology, papers scattering everywhere.

To the people living under the thumb of Ephesus and Rome, Paul declares that the same power that raised Jesus from the dead is *theirs*. No one else—not the Emperor, not Artemis— had been resurrected from the dead and seated at the right hand of God. However bleak the Christian community's economic, social, or political outlook may have been, Paul doesn't pray for their safety (suffering was all but certain). He prays for their faith, their hope, and their love—and he does so while suffering himself.

Paul can't keep his eyes on the ground, can't stay focused on all the reasons to be afraid. Paul is distracted from fear by good news.

EMPIRE CHRISTIANS

Today, I write from "the most powerful nation on earth."[10] Our government, economy, and religious leaders have unequaled power in this world. But like the Christians of Ephesus, we cannot bow before that government, cannot be ruled by that economy, cannot be formed by religious celebrities. We have only one King: the resurrected Jesus. We follow the God of love, and we should be known by that love.

But are we, really?

We generally identify Christ followers by looking for the word *Christian*. But God says nothing about distinguishing us by our label—God says his children will be recognized *by our love*. The church survived centuries of social marginalization and legal persecution and cannot be stopped from the outside. But we will annihilate ourselves from the inside if we are too afraid to practice God's love—to lay down our rights and our lives, if necessary, in service to our neighbors, strangers, and enemies.

That's why Paul and his friends were so empowered. They were never safe or privileged. But when God raised Jesus from the dead, he so entirely vindicated Jesus' Kingdom, so completely rewrote the rules of life on earth, so clearly demonstrated his end game of new creation, that there was no longer any reason to be afraid. What could a mere human do to you? With the insight of the Holy Spirit, the early Christians looked at Jesus' resurrection and concluded something earth-shattering, something strong enough to fold history in two. They believed that Jesus was the firstfruits, the early harvest of redemption, a down payment on the promise that God would resurrect Jesus' followers too. The cycle of new life had begun before their eyes, and they were invited to partner with God to bring it to pass. They had "died with Christ"[11] and no longer lived for themselves but for the Kingdom. All of humankind was being redeemed, all of creation.

Where then, was fear? What could earthly kings do, if Jesus had been crowned the true King, if God's love and justice were declared the final word? The fearmongers of this world could no longer hold these men and women. These Empire Christians had nothing to fear from the brutal powers that threatened their lives.

The question these first Christians answered so definitively comes back around to us today. We are empire Christians, too, dual citizens of the modern world and the Kingdom of God. Have we caught the vision of a love that goes beyond the grave? What king do we bow before—and whom do we fear?

CHAPTER 3

FEARING GOD

I WALKED INTO MY FIRST COLLEGE WORSHIP SERVICE with all the jittery excitement of a brand-new freshman. Scanning the room for new friends, I walked toward an open seat as the lyrics of the song we were singing slowly trickled into my consciousness:

Purify my heart
Let me be as gold and precious silver
Purify my heart
Let me be as gold, pure gold

Refiner's fire
My heart's one desire
Is to be holy
Set apart for You, Lord[1]

This was the first time I had heard this song—and I was appalled. A few hundred teenagers and young adults were reading words off a screen, casually and passively asking to be put through fire. I had undergone some life-altering suffering in my life by then and had an inkling what it felt like to be burnt down and rebuilt. But did they? No way would I blithely repeat these words simply because they appeared on a screen; no chance would I plead for God to take me through fires so hot and long-standing that I would be permanently altered. This is a worthwhile prayer, of course, but one to enter with intentionality, discernment, and community while counting the cost. I could not imagine doing so without lying on my face, trembling with the weight of it.

To this day, I have never sung the words to this song on demand.

Two years after this worship service, I was in a car accident. Lying on the ground outside the passenger door, waiting for the ambulance to arrive, I realized that my roommate's mixtape was still playing from the crumpled metal of the dashboard. The garbled words coming through the speakers were the same ones I'd heard that night of worship: *Refiner's fire, my heart's one desire is to be holy.* The cassette itself was in the process of being burned, but it played one last time. Lying there in crisis and pain, I felt more at peace than I could remember ever feeling before. God encompassed my entire being, pointed to my fear, and said, "See? This is the lesson. You're not *safe*, but I'm with you."

WORSHIP AND FEAR

God announced the birth of his new nation at Mount Sinai, speaking loudly enough for the folks on the ground to hear. And not only hear: This was a multimedia event! Thunder and lightning ricocheted around camp. The mountain quaked, billowing smoke as trumpets sounded through the din. Everyone was horrified, keeping their distance, trembling with terror. Then Moses said, "Do not be afraid. God has come to test you, so that the fear of God will be with you."[2]

Wait, what now?

Do not be afraid, for God is bringing you the fear of God. In addition to being terrified out of their minds, these folks can be forgiven for feeling completely confused. As often as God commands us to not fear, the Bible admonishes us to fear God— sometimes in the same breath. So, which is it? Should we fear or not fear? Is this simply nonsense?

As my seminary professor likes to say, what looks like contradictions in Scripture are often clues pointing us toward the real treasure if we are willing to dig for it. Apparent inconsistency may be a chance to learn something important about a complex God.[3] When we dig into these two statements about fear, we find ourselves uncovering the secret to love.

The word translated "fear" (of the Lord) is the Hebrew word *yir'â*, which can mean terror but also reverence and awe. This is a reasonable response to God's transcendence. But fearing God does not mean looking over our shoulders lest judgement and wrath overtake us. Instead, fearing God means putting God's love, compassion, and power in their proper place. We overcome our fears of lesser powers by worshiping true goodness, surrendering to the Creator, the faithful Alpha and Omega. When we revere God, we realize that the path of life comes from him, and through him, and to him. We focus our eyes on God's face, not on the waves around us.

When we "fear" God, God's plan for goodness, love, and redemption becomes our driving force and goal. With God's Kingdom taking up so much space in our minds, we feed on messages of hope, not terror. This discipline rewires our brain pathways, literally "renewing our minds," as Paul says.[4]

In other words, God's call throughout Scripture to un-fear becomes possible when we rewire our brains to live in reverence of God. This is a posture of worship, submitting ourselves to our trustworthy and faithful Creator, our loving parent. Jesus does not invite us to live safe lives; neither does he invite us to live in constant terror. Jesus invites us to place our eyes on God and walk forward into the storm.

There's a flip side to this, and it warrants close attention: When we don't practice the worship and reverence of the loving Creator God, we begin to worship what we do fear. We will serve, align to, and be formed into the image of our fears over time. We create idols of fear, doctrines and religions of fear. We become discipled daily by fear, learning to serve and worship fear, following fear as our teacher and lord. The conversion may happen so slowly and organically that we continue using the word *Christianity* to describe our worship; we may still call on the name of Jesus when addressing these idols. But what we practice, embody, and bring to life in our communities will not be in line with God's Kingdom.

AFRAID OF GOD

When the people pushed away from the smoke and fire around Mount Sinai, God exhorted them to turn from fear and toward "the fear of God"—rewiring their response by realigning to

God's redemptive plan, following the path of life through worship and reverence. But even with the mountain quaking, it was touch and go for centuries. So often they chose to build idols they could touch and control, to worship the gods who demanded blood and violence but promised prosperity and comfort in return.

The choice before us today is no less stark: Will we follow the violent, greedy gods we have built in a fearful attempt to protect ourselves and gain prosperity? Or will we repent and turn to God? Will we worship and revere Jesus the Christ and our Lord, laying down our rights and our lives to follow the resurrected Jesus in a life of radical love to anyone who is our neighbor, stranger, or enemy? (There aren't many humans on the planet not included in that trifecta.)

Do we fear God more than we fear our idols? The question haunts me. Even now, after the resurrection, do we who identify as followers of Jesus place our identity in him so thoroughly that we find courage to love our neighbors, strangers, and enemies—and change the world by risking love?

But another question haunts me even more—are we *afraid* of God? I wonder if our underlying problem is that we would prefer to follow a god who is more concerned with our personal wealth and comfort, who holds a preference for "us" over "them." I suspect we are afraid to follow the God who died for his enemies, who seeks victory by relinquishing power, who sets free through love rather than destruction. Are we afraid to love the God who invites his followers to die rather than kill?

The first Christ followers were Jews who had awaited a messiah for centuries. Messiah would come in power and glory, like a king, and set things right again. In the midst of this ancient hope, the Jewish Christians proclaimed a genuinely unbelievable message: Jesus of Nazareth was that long-awaited Messiah.

But there was a major problem staring them in the face: Their Messiah had been killed. Even the Resurrection didn't solve this difficulty, for honor was the measure of one's worth in the ancient world. Jesus underwent extreme humiliation and the shame of public defeat at the hands of the empire, before the eyes of everyone. As we saw earlier, crucifixion was calculated not only for severe physical suffering but maximum public shame. Such humiliation was insurmountable for someone claiming to be victorious, to be from God. Deuteronomy 21:23 says "cursed of God is the one who has been hanged on a tree."[5]

So, no. For them, it was obvious: Jesus was not the Messiah. The Messiah could not be cursed of God, could not suffer. Jesus suffered. Jesus was utterly dishonored, executed, hung on a cross. Jesus was not the Messiah.

But when Mark wrote his gospel, he was saying, "Look at this! We missed it! Jesus is the Messiah after all—check this out!" Looking back at the prophets, and at Jesus' own teaching, Mark demonstrates that the Messiah they were waiting for was a suffering Messiah. This was good news for Mark's readers: They didn't need to be ashamed of following a leader, a God, who publicly suffered humiliation and apparent failure, who would lay down his life, who would win through weakness, who would gain victory through death.

But the reality of the suffering Messiah was and remains a stumbling block, because as his followers, we must be willing to go down the same path, the path of suffering, humiliation, and death.

Listen to these words from Mark:

[Jesus] then began to **teach them that the Son of Man must suffer many things** and be rejected by the elders, the chief priests and the teachers of the law, and that he must be killed and after three days rise again. He spoke plainly about this, and **Peter took him aside and began to rebuke him.**

But when Jesus turned and looked at his disciples, he rebuked Peter. "Get behind me, Satan!" he said. "You do not have in mind the concerns of God, but merely human concerns."

Then he called the crowd to him along with his disciples and said: "Whoever wants to be my disciple must deny themselves and take up their cross and follow me. **For whoever wants to save their life will lose it, but whoever loses their life for me and for the gospel will save it.** What good is it for someone to gain the whole world, yet forfeit their soul? Or what can anyone give in exchange for their soul? **If anyone is ashamed of me** and my words in this adulterous and sinful generation, the Son of Man will be ashamed of them when he comes in his Father's glory with the holy angels."[6]

This passage make sense when we listen through the ears of the honor-bound early Christians, suffering persecution for following a humiliated messiah. To them, Mark's theology was earthshaking. It was world-changing good news.

And us today? With Peter, we like to stand by the powerful. Perhaps we create God in our own image because we would prefer not to follow a God who was crucified, who calls us to lay down our lives for our friends and enemies.

The God of Scripture does not cause suffering but suffers for the sake of others, overcoming fear and hatred with love. This is the opposite of what we're comfortable with, what we consider "right." Are we afraid to surrender to a God who asks this of himself, and of us? Would we rather be afraid than love?

Something about Jesus' good news renders *safety* no longer the most important thing. The Kingdom is what we're after, now. So the question is this: Do you want to follow Jesus and find this love that surpasses safety, the only force strong enough to short-circuit our wiring toward fear and hate?

SAVED BY GRACE

As we grapple with submitting to a God who invites us to come and die, there's another layer of fear that often scares us away from God. For generations, our definition of *Christian* has been overshadowed by medieval threats of eternal damnation.[7] Many view God as an abusive parent who can never be pleased or placated. Many of us were offered good news through a disguise of horrible news: that we are so worthless God can barely tolerate us, that Jesus is somehow sneaking us into the family in an unmarked box labeled "grace." Condemnation feels so close at hand. When we hear that God has work for us to do, we panic. *What if we fail? What if we fall short?* Or conversely, we shut the whole idea down: *No, I'm saved by grace. God knows better than to expect anything from me.*

Rarely do we ask ourselves, *What is God forming this family for? Is there something God is sending us out to do?* It's a scary question, because if God expects us to live in a particular way and complete a challenging mission during our time on earth, it's all too easy to imagine God's displeasure nipping at our heels.

But God isn't the abusive, punitive parent we often imagine. God's grace is about so much more than letting Jesus sneak us into the family.

The word we translate *grace* is the Greek word *charis*. Grace, as we know, refers to the unmerited gift of God's loving-kindness; it is through grace we are saved. Our life and breath and relationship with God are all gifts, something we could never earn. But in the Greco-Roman world of Jesus and Paul, *charis* was part of a complex social system. A wealthy patron would offer gifts and resources to someone far lower in society. These gifts could not be earned, and certainly never repaid. But by accepting the gift of grace, the recipient agreed to remain in an ongoing, reciprocal relationship with the wealthy patron. It was understood and accepted that they would pivot their lives toward benefiting each other.

So when Paul writes of God's grace to us, God's *charis*, he absolutely means that God gives us life, love, acceptance, and salvation out of his kindness—and there's not a thing we could do to earn or deserve it, much less pay it back. But in Paul's time and place, everyone also understood that, having received the offered gift, we owe our lives to God. Not because God is holding our heavy burden of debt over our heads like a mob boss—it was a gift given in love—but because we have entered into a relationship with strong ties that bind us joyfully and deeply together. Now what God wants, we want, and we work together to achieve, continuously supported by this intimate relationship called grace.

This understanding of grace is even more wonderful and compelling than we usually imagine. We obey God and work for God not because we are afraid God cannot love us but *because we have been bound together in a relationship of love.*

The Bible, from Genesis to Jesus, tells of God selecting a few people and calling them to follow and serve him. But never is the calling for their own blessing or salvation; always the blessing is for the entire world, the whole community. Some are chosen, predestined, but not for their own gain: Our election is to a committee of servants called *the church*, the body of Christ in the world, who love our neighbors, serve the strangers, and care even for our enemies—bringing God's redemption to *all*. God doesn't love only a few; God loves the whole world. Jesus doesn't guard the door to God—Jesus throws open the door. Christians are not primarily individuals who have been spared punishment from an angry deity but a community of people who have subverted the powers of fear and death by dying with Christ and rising with Christ to live and work for the Kingdom.

So let's get this out of the way, once and for all: Are you loved by God? Does God want to be in a relationship with you? Is God present and active in your life? The answer is a resounding *YES*. It has always been yes. It will always be yes.

This yes has nothing to do with what you've done or not done. In infinite, abounding love, God creates, nurtures, and sustains out of love. If the sparrows are known and accounted for, if the flowers in the field are cultivated with compassion, *so are you.*

So then, in this place of safety and significance, there is another question for you to consider: Will you follow Jesus? Following Jesus is about far more than what we think or believe— following changes what we *do, how we live.* Discipleship doesn't ask us to merely convert our beliefs but to get up and move, to become and behave in a different way. To accept the gift and pledge your life to the giver. Jesus invites you to take up your cross and join a community of people who are working for the source of grace, not out of debt or fear of damnation but out of joyful, safe, loving relationship.

Where could fear possibly exist when we have been encompassed in such a life-altering love?

Every person, butterfly, lizard, and guppy is loved and cherished by God. There is more than enough of God's presence to go around. But *Christians* are the group of people whose individual lives have been surrendered to a relationship and assigned to a team on mission.

Like the disciples, we must choose what path to follow: fear and hate, or love and compassion? Will we love our neighbors as ourselves, care for the stranger, and pray for our enemies? As I realized at that freshman-year worship service, this is not a decision to take lightly; we should not join in simply because everyone around us is going along. Discipleship is an active decision that will lead us into fire, that will burn away what we have clung to and worshiped and loved.

Fear and hate will certainly not make us safer—but a life of love may not either. Fearing God enough to follow God's path of love might lead us directly into the jaws of danger and death. But only one of these paths is the way of the Kingdom.

BRAVE STEPS

"FEAR NOT" ISN'T A MATTER OF AGREEMENT—this is a way of living, an embodied choice to turn our lives over to God again, and again, and again. Whether you are reading alone or with a group, take some time with these questions, practices, and activities to discern what role fear plays in your life and what it might look like to "fear not" in your community.

REFLECT AND DISCUSS

What are you afraid of?

In what ways does fear hold you back?

From what sources do you hear messages that feed your fears or encourage you to distrust or fear something or someone (or a group of someones)?

What do you think of the evidence that Christians are known for their fear, rather than for their love?

What is it about Jesus' good news that empowers his followers to go to unsafe places and do unsafe things, yet live out of love rather than fear? What do you think that could look like in your life, church, or community?

Are you afraid of God? How does that play out in your life and faith?

PRACTICE

- Create a safe and comfortable space and spend some time considering this question: *What am I afraid of?* You may prefer silence or soft music in the background. Ask God to reveal fears you may not be aware of. Make a list or draw pictures as they come to mind.

   Next, gently investigate your fears after you have identified them. Where do they come from? Are they based in prior hurts and trauma? Are they based in potential losses? Are they fed by the media or messages in your community? In what ways have these fears kept you safe? In what ways are they holding you back?

   Finally, release your fears to God. Find a way to do this tangibly. For example, write them on slips of paper and toss them, one by one, into a bonfire. Or gather a handful of pebbles and sit by a river, pond, lake, or ocean. Name each fear as you release a pebble deep into the water.

- How do you view God? Color a picture that depicts God as you imagine God; the point is not to do this "right" or be theologically correct but to understand what images and beliefs guide your unconscious thoughts. What did you draw, and why? Where did this view come from? Is it helpful or unhelpful? Then, consider and write a response for the following prompts:

  - What images and ideas of God am I being invited to let go of?

  - What images and ideas of God am I being invited to consider and welcome?

LOOK AND LISTEN

- *The Hand of God* painting by Yongsung Kim
- "Slow Your Breath Down" song by Future of Forestry
- "No Longer a Slave" song by Bethel Music

Find this art or music online, then spend time sitting with it. What do you see and hear? What invitation is God offering you through them?

SECTION TWO

NEIGHBORS

*We should respond to our neighbors . . . not in proportion
to what we see as their due but in proportion to their need.
The cost to us personally should count for nothing.*

HUSTON SMITH

WHEN JESUS TRAVELED HIS HOMELAND OF GALILEE, preaching and teaching the Kingdom of God, the community began to gather. He walked through villages and along the lake, getting into the boats and saying to the listening crowds, "The time has come! Turn back to God, for the kingdom of heaven is near!"[1]

Could it be? Could this man, their own neighbor, return the children of Israel to their land, their king, their kingdom? Could this be the long-awaited Messiah?

It's preposterous, of course. Not Jesus of Nazareth, whom they have known since childhood. But who doesn't want to hang around and listen—at least to see what he'll do next?

What he does next is approach two brothers in their boat, on the lake, casting their nets for fish. It's good work, fishing. Not prestigious or flashy, but a chance to put food on the table and a roof over your family's head. There will always be hungry people; there will always be fish in the sea.

Jesus watches them work, then calls out.

"Simon! Andrew! Leave your nets. Come follow me."[2]

Farther down the lakeshore, Jesus sees two more brothers, James and John, and extends the same invitation.

These four men must have been a bit hesitant, maybe even afraid of such an enormous change. Who wouldn't be? But they did it; they left their boats and nets. They left their plans, their livelihood and family home, and followed. Hearing Jesus' words—they had done that for years. Wrestling with his teaching, discussing it, concluding finally that his words were true—they had done all that too. But now, today, they were invited to leave their lives behind and follow. This meant action, movement, change. They were disciples now. Their task was to work with their bodies—just as they had worked with nets and boats—and join a team fishing for people, for the Kingdom.

And they did. All throughout Galilee they went with Jesus, talking with their neighbors, teaching the good news, healing those who were sick, providing for those who had needs. Even the paralyzed began to walk again. Jesus taught and healed, healed and taught. He taught many things, but said it all could be summarized in two commands: Love God, and love your neighbor.

Maybe for some this was a matter of the heart. Maybe some in the crowd nodded in agreement and went home with their hearts a bit more worshipful, more compassionate. But for the disciples who reoriented their lives around following Jesus, this was not a theoretical idea, a task to work out in their head and heart. These four brothers—and many more—didn't just listen to Jesus' words and agree with them. They followed. They worked. Loving God and their neighbor was what they did, now. The kingdom was worthy of their entire lives.

CHAPTER 4

NEXT-DOOR STRANGERS

I HAD JUST CHANGED INTO COZY PAJAMA PANTS when I heard the first siren, but the fire truck barreling down the street barely registered in my mind. We live a block from the station and hear them all the time. But then came another, and another, and I realized they were not leaving but arriving. More than a dozen, not just from our local fire station but from all the surrounding districts as well. Slipping on a pair of sandals, I headed out the door to see what I could see.

What I saw was a house down the street on fire, the flames bright and terrifying against the dark night sky. Dozens of us came out of our doors, meeting at the police line we could not cross, mingling in the night air. As the fire raged, we stood in our pajamas for hours, asking and answering questions: *Is everyone okay? Does anyone know who lives there? Does anyone know what happened?* We scrolled through Facebook for news, trading tidbits of information.

The thing was, few of us knew the residents of this house, this family who lived among us. We didn't even know one another. These next-door neighbors were mostly strangers to me and to each other. As we watched and waited and worried, we swapped stories—where we had gone to college, where we worked or worshiped, how many kids we had and where they went to school. We were surprised that we had so much in common, that we had lived here all these years, that we had never met until now.

That was over a year ago. Now, when I take my evening walks through town, I pass the same houses and think how strange it is that I still don't know who lives there, even though we spent the night talking all those months ago. Even as I wave to the folks sitting on their porches or working in the yard, I don't recognize them from that dark night in our pj's or remember which story fits which face. For one night we gathered out of shared curiosity but then went back into our separate buildings—so close and yet so far away.

CHARITY BEGINS AT HOME

When Jesus was asked to summarize what practices and theologies were most important to God, out of all the commands and rituals inside his long, rich faith tradition, he chose two: Love God with everything you are, and love your neighbor as yourself. This is what God wants most from us. Not travel the world on mission, not become a celebrity teacher, not gain more followers, not raise money to sponsor a new church building, not memorize and recite all the right verses, not even subscribe to correct doctrine. *Love God. Love your neighbor as yourself.*

During my decades in the church, I have seen folks separate from other Christians who disagree about the dates and mechanism of the beginning or ending of the world, the literal versus metaphorical meaning of Genesis and Revelation. I have seen differing interpretations and translations of Bible verses on sexuality, gender roles, or politics lead earnest disciples of Jesus to conclude that other earnest disciples are not, in fact, *real* Christians but tools of the devil. Yet I have never seen anyone's feet truly held to the fire with questions such as: Are you loving your neighbors? Actively? Sacrificially? Are you reading this verse literally? Do you love your neighbors as you love yourself?

Jesus might think this is the most important command, the one that ensures we are walking in God's will—but we don't seem to think so.

Those of us who choose to follow the resurrected Jesus are invited—no, commanded—to love our neighbors.[1] Charity begins at home, as they say—meaning, don't feed your pride by publicly doing good works if you won't take the time and energy to feed those closest to you. This seems like such a no-brainer. *Of course* we should take care of our own. And for most of history, neighbors were extended family, your own tribe. There was little sense of "me" but a strong sense of "we." Folks lived or died together in community. *Of course* they loved their neighbors as they loved themselves. Loving neighbors *was* loving themselves; their neighbors *were* themselves.

But this gets tricky for Americans. Ours is a highly mobile and isolated society, built upon individual autonomy. Our sense of self—as well as our time, money, and energy—points inward. We don't expect our lives to be interdependent with our parents or adult children, much less everyone within walking distance. Plus, there is no clear path to wealth or fame in a life lived close to home. Let's check that box and move on to bigger, riskier, more applause-worthy tasks. No one cheers or even notices if I care for those in my local community.

A recent Pew Research Study found that just over 50 percent of Americans know some of their neighbors; only a quarter know most, while a quarter of adults under age thirty say they know none of their neighbors. But even those who selected "some" or "most" reported they rarely socialize or interact face-to-face.[2]

As an American follower of Jesus, do I prioritize his number-one command and love my neighbors? To be honest, I don't actively set out to harm them, but I don't love them as I love myself. I love most of my neighbors as I love my fourth cousin on my dad's side: mild interest, certainly no ill-will, but almost zero knowledge or engagement. Any love I have is purely theoretical.

PRACTICING *AGAPĒ*

When translators render pronouns from the Bible into English, they run into grammar problems. When we read the word *you* in English, we assume it is singular—in other words, one person. But English cannot differentiate between an individual or collective *you*. This one word could refer to me alone, or the entire forty-thousand-person crowd in Wrigley Field; that's a big difference. And in fact, nearly all second-person pronouns in the New Testament are plural. Jesus and the apostles were not commanding, teaching, and encouraging *you*. They were talking to *y'all*. Not *Catherine* or *Carlos* but *all of you guys together as a group*.

This one seemingly tiny English-translation limitation has tremendous impact on our theology and the ways we practice our faith. When our understanding of sin, redemption, and salvation is centered on the individual, we miss the point. The gospel is primarily a group situation, less "Look at what God did for *me!*" and more "Look at what God did for *us!*"[3] Following Jesus and obeying God changes from expectations placed on *me* to a group project given to *us*—a community working as we fellowship together. The heavy burden of loving our neighbors becomes easy with many hands to lighten the load.

But reading Jesus' and the apostles' teachings correctly— much less seriously following them—is hard for us English-speaking Americans. We want the gospel message to be primarily for us as individuals, but it isn't. The good news never was and never will be just for *me*. The good news is for *us*.

So let's consider the implications of reading the command "Love your neighbor as yourself." Most of us have read it as "*You* love the man or woman next door as you love *yourself*." But Jesus is really saying, "*You all* care for your community the way you care for *your own family*."[4]

Does that feel like a mic-drop moment to you? It does to me. This moves the command from countercultural to life-altering.

Maybe that's why we don't hold ourselves to this standard. Loving our neighbors sounds so simple, but living it out requires the full upheaval of our lives. It means moving outside our comfort zones and intentionally messing up our carefully ordered existence with people we might not like or enjoy. Caring for our community will require us to share our resources—money, time, and energy. Our identity and goals must shift from being for us as individuals to *us* as part of a group. Loving our neighbors this way is simply not how we expected to structure our homes, families, or lives—and, understandably, we prefer a Christianity that does not require so much investment and sacrifice.

Yet the early church understood what Jesus meant. In his letter to the believers, James implores us not to be "double-minded," agreeing with the wisdom of Jesus yet not *doing* the wisdom of Jesus.[5] The question for would-be disciples—then and now—is not if we *agree* with Jesus, but if we will *follow*.

The early Christians re-formed their lives around caring for the whole community as their own family, an active love Paul described as *agapē*. In his letters, Paul teaches that the ongoing practice of agapē is central to the Christian identity: not a feeling of love but a communal life founded on respect, service, help, and solidarity.[6] Fellow Christians would be bound together with agapē, but the community living outside the faith would benefit too.[7] The book of Acts describes the believers' habit of meeting together daily, and eating meals together—which was scandalous in a way we struggle to understand, given the strict ethnic, religious, and socioeconomic boundaries they crossed to do so. When anyone in the community had a need, someone else with means would provide, even selling land or property if necessary.[8] Justin Martyr, writing around AD 150, described the massive redistribution of wealth that was part and parcel of Christian worship: After celebrating the Lord's Supper together, those who had enough presented their resources to the group, which was used to "[succor] the orphans and widows and those who, through sickness or any other cause, are in want, and those who are in bonds and the strangers sojourning among us."[9] A century later, Dionysus wrote that during the plague, Christians did not flee from their sick neighbors as most citizens did, leaving them to die alone while they saved themselves. Rather "most of our brethren were unsparing in their exceeding love and brotherly kindness. They held fast to each other and visited the sick fearlessly, and ministered to them continually, serving them in Christ. And they died with them most joyfully, taking the affliction of others, and drawing the sickness from their neighbors to themselves and willingly receiving their pains."[10]

Death had no more power over these followers of Christ, so what was left to fear? What power—since greed and selfish gain had been sacrificed with Christ—could hold them back from loving their community of neighbors? As the author of 1 John wrote, "If anyone has material possessions and sees a brother or sister in need but has no pity on them, how can the love of God be in that person?"[11]

How indeed? I wonder how deeply our world would be soothed if, after sharing Communion each week, Christians still pooled their resources to ensure that no one in the community lacked food, shelter, or education; that visitors moving into town were welcomed and provided for—even if it meant we made room in our own houses or sold property to make it so. If, instead of fearing the habits, beliefs, and diseases of our neighbors, our active, agapē love left no oxygen for fear. If we cared about the literal meaning of verses like these.

This would require us to listen to and learn from our brothers and sisters—next door, across town, across the tracks—and form a family, a group identity, sharing together in our suffering *and* in our hope for redemption. We would learn to see ourselves not as "me" but part of "us," perceiving the suffering of our neighbors as our own suffering. Rather than grieving the loss of our vacation funds or the sale of our second car, we would celebrate that the man across town could afford his cancer treatments, that the newly arriving immigrant families had secure shelter and could meet their basic needs, that the single mom was able to keep her job *and* know her kids were safe. We could let go of our resources without fear of the future, knowing that our own needs would be met in community as well.

Following Jesus requires us to release our privilege and stand in solidarity. We become invested in what happens to our community, to society, and to the country because the injustice and suffering isn't happening to *them* but to *us*. Never mind that I don't feel the pain myself: My sister felt it, my brother felt it. *We* felt it. *We* will stand together and fight for healing.

This is what it means to be a neighbor. This is what it means to be a Christian.

WE'LL LEAVE THE LIGHTS ON

I often think of Jesus' description of his followers as "the salt of the world."[12] In ancient times, salt was essential. In a culture with hot temperatures and no refrigeration, salt kept meat and food from spoiling, killed bacteria, and slowed the process of rot. Salt preserved by holding inevitable decomposition at bay. Before antibiotics, salt was used to stop deadly infection from setting in a wound. And of course, we all know how salt draws out flavor, taking a dish from bland to delicious.

So, Jesus describes his followers this way: giving flavor to the world and keeping it healthy, slowing the process of infection and death. Followers of Christ influence communities by actively contributing to long-term health.

But too much salt in a dish renders it unpalatable. The intensity of industrial-strength salt kills living things. Come spring where I live, after months of winter, salt trucks have done their work: Patches of dead grass are left along the side of the roads. Jesus' metaphor only works when many tiny grains of salt—too insignificant on their own to do much of anything at all—work together toward something greater than the sum of its parts.

This is what happens when Jesus' followers take him seriously about loving neighbors. When we live for ourselves, by ourselves, we are useless. When we huddle up in a big group, not dispersing beyond our own careful borders, we become useless then, too—or deadly. But sprinkled here and there and everywhere, we contribute to health and wholeness, simply by caring for the community where we are, as a million other Jesus-followers do the same.

Jesus went on to pronounce his followers "the light of the world." In the original Greek language, the words are spoken with emphasis—*you are the light of the world!* Imagine ancient times before electricity, when roughly half of each day is darkness. No streetlamps or light bulbs reveal what may be hiding in shadows; relief comes only from the far-off dawn. If there was a light—a candle or an oil lamp—it must be placed prominently to brighten the widest possible area. Followers of Christ, in other words, shine the light of Christ to the benefit of many, not hide it for ourselves. *My* tiny light need not save the whole world, but if I join it with others in my community, we make our neighborhood safer and more beautiful.

Think of a neighborhood blazing with Christmas lights, how the glittering incandescence takes your breath away. That's how the Kingdom of God comes to earth, one tiny light, one community at a time. When a billion people around the globe do the same in their neighborhoods, we light up the whole world.

Jesus was not teaching people in powerful or wealthy positions. He wasn't even addressing his inner circle of disciples. Jesus was talking to *the crowd*. Profoundly ordinary folks, residents of Galilee and the surrounding areas: fishermen, tradesmen, mothers and fathers, aunties and uncles, regular people in every respect. Yet these average men and women are the ones empowered to stop the earth from sinking into darkness and rot, to protect their communities from infection, flavorlessness, and decay—simply by each being salt and light in their one tiny corner, by faithfully loving their closest neighbors.

In today's world, we have refrigerators and twenty-four-hour electric lights to keep our food and sidewalks safe. We expect social change and the public good to come from elected officials and nonprofit organizations. Yet suffering and injustice still permeate our communities. Perhaps it is time to try Jesus' strategy: ordinary people around the world actively caring for their neighbors. If we were serious about putting our backs to this practice of agapē love, we might start seeing a planet preserved from its own decay, a place where God's will is done as in heaven. That's what Jesus said, anyway. We are each one candle in one window, and together we provide safety and light for the whole city.[13]

––––––––––––––

Walking through my neighborhood, I see how each house forms a kingdom of its own, together encompassing an empire of individuals—and I realize how difficult it is for us to step out of our individual kingdoms and live for the Kingdom of God. How do we break out of the mold of individual autonomy and our growing fear of our neighbors (if we think about them at all) and restructure our lives around agapē love *practiced in* community? Caring for our neighbors is both the lowest bar and the highest bar Jesus offers us, the full summary of his request to us, his people.

We begin by knowing those near us, one small-but-brave step at a time. In the United States, 240 million people consider themselves Christians. If each one of us committed to investing in our neighborhoods, loving the community in the same way we love ourselves, nearly everyone would be looked after. Those of us who are hungry would be fed, those of us who are lonely would be enveloped by family, those of us who are afraid would find friends who have their backs.

Sometimes the most complex problems have the simplest solutions. Is it possible Jesus knew what he was talking about when he said that everything in the Law and Prophets could be summarized by loving God and loving our neighbor?

CHAPTER 5

WHO ARE THE PEOPLE IN YOUR NEIGHBORHOOD?

IT'S MONDAY NIGHT AT 6:00 P.M., which means I'm running out of the house, carrying a hot pan straight off the stove, one child racing ahead to open the doors, another following behind me with a serving spoon. We're eating dinner with neighbors tonight, just down the road. With several neighbors, in fact.

A few years ago, some of us within walking distance began a tradition called Messy Monday. Each Monday our households eat dinner together as a spiritual practice. We are not allowed to clean the house in advance or prepare a fancy meal; we simply open up our lives and spaces as is, a work in progress. Everyone brings whatever they would have eaten that night anyway, whether a fancy dish or blue-box mac-'n-cheese. Practicing this discipline means letting people see the state of our houses and lives, the reality of shared leftovers confronting our worship of independence and autonomy. It's a small way to practice love over fear.

But as I nibble potluck remnants at the kitchen counter (the table and chairs were already taken), one thing is glaringly obvious to me: I would have been friends with these people anyway. Our shared background, religion, education, and skin color set us up to be kindred spirits. In this multicultural city and diverse country, my neighbors originally hail from all over the world. What are the odds I would live near people so similar to myself?

Actually, the odds are extremely high. Most Americans live among people of the same or similar race, religion, educational level, and socioeconomic status.[1] This is even more likely to be true for white Americans like myself. Loving and serving our communities as God intends is hard enough, given how rarely we know our neighbors, how focused we are on individual identity. But Jesus' command requires more than hosting barbeques and sharing Christmas cookies. We must take a step back and consider why we reside near certain kinds of people and not near others. Not only *Who is my neighbor?* but also—*Why?*

POWERFUL PROXIMITY

There is power in proximity.[2] Where we live and work and go to church, where we shop, where we send our kids to school, who we rub shoulders with day in and day out—these choices matter. Even if the decision to live "here" instead of "there" seems unconscious or outside our immediate control, it does not happen by accident. Neither are the factors morally neutral or inconsequential. What makes us consider one community desirable and another undesirable? How does this influence our posture of love over fear? The people we bump into regularly impact our knowledge and empathy, influencing who we suspect and who we understand. So, to love as God commands, we must consider the dynamics behind who is and isn't our neighbor.[3]

When I listen to Christians give advice regarding where to live and who to mingle with, nearly every message I hear is a warning. I find this especially true when speaking with other middle-class Christians like myself. Whether we are afraid of race, poverty, immigration status, sexual orientation, religion, secularism, or fundamentalism, decisions about proximity seem to be weighed primarily out of a fear of danger, rather than considering what Jesus might ask of us. We talk about wanting a *good* neighborhood, *good* schools, and a *good* church—which implies we don't want the *bad* neighborhoods, *bad* schools, or *bad* churches. But what does *good* mean in this context? Good for whom? Good for what? If the answer is "Good for using my privilege to give my family every possible leg up in the world," that is a valid choice for an American. But for Christians? Jesus commands us to care for the community as we care for our own families. We cannot be the salt and light Jesus sends us out to be if we segregate, if we spend what we have been given on ourselves or on those who already have everything we have.

Depending on your context, your fears and decisions may unfold differently; your Christian community will have unique challenges to wrestle through together. But no matter who or where we are, we are called to look upon our communities with the eyes, heart, and mind of Christ.

I am intrigued by God's command to the exiles in Babylon to "seek the peace and prosperity of the city to which I have carried you into exile."[4] Without a doubt, these folks lived in a hostile culture. Can you imagine being carried away as a hostage and forced to live in the nation that upended your way of life, that destroyed your family and country? The exiles worked day and night to maintain their unique identity, to be "a peculiar people" and not adopt foreign values and lifestyles. Yet even with this ever-present danger, even though Babylon was their literal mortal enemy, they were commanded by God to not only consider what was good for themselves but work for the benefit of the city.

Take a moment to picture yourself in the shoes of these exiles. Can you imagine? Talk about being unsafe. Yet God required them to choose love and service over fear.

If this was God's heart for the families abducted to Babylon, surely he wants us to seek the good of the city where we reside, to consider how our decisions impact the peace and prosperity of those around us. We are afraid of godless agendas and dangerous neighborhoods—but our "godless" neighbor is not where the risk to our Christian values lies. In choosing to exercise our own rights and seek our own individual good over the good of our neighbors, we have already been infiltrated by America's secular values at the expense of God's Kingdom.

Of course, this is a two-way street. If we are afraid to mingle with certain parts of our community, they're likely scared of us too. We've sent clear and powerful signals that we aren't trustworthy, that we don't see them as equals or value them. A major trust breach develops over time—one that isn't easily mended.

When we choose the opposite path, inviting people to join our lives, families, and homes until our paths irrevocably mingle, it does change us—but that's not something to be afraid of. Relationships are powerful, but that doesn't mean they're dangerous. Viewing life's realities through the eyes of people we love forms us on a level that books and education cannot reach. When we hear life stories and testimonies from neighbors while watching their faces and eyes, touching their hands— then their experiences become intertwined with ours. Our stories become intertwined with theirs. We become a "we," not an "us-and-them."

Remember, in the last chapter, when we imagined communities using their resources to ensure everyone could get by? I've seen people live like that—but rarely in the "good" neighborhoods. Rather, it's in the less-affluent communities where I've witnessed this Kingdom-living thrive, where my neighbors have taught me how to place value in my fellow humans rather than in my possessions and net worth. How much Kingdom goodness do we miss out on, in the name of choosing a so-called "better life" for our families?

Our isolation may be unwitting, yet this makes it hard for us to step into the blessing and suffering of our brothers and sisters, and for them to share in our blessings and help in our sufferings. When we live among those who are like us—racially, ethnically, religiously, educationally, economically—we withhold something important from ourselves, something we don't even realize we are missing: intimacy and cross-pollination with people who are different from us.

GOD'S LAND

I sat at a small conference table, sipping tea and interviewing people for a feature-length article. A large and well-resourced church nearby had spent ten years and millions of dollars investing in the local community: teaching English as a second language, teaching adults to read and write for the first time, helping kids succeed at school, being a well-resourced friend during times of crisis, being good neighbors to the community. Now, to celebrate ten years of beautiful relationship-building, I was sent to interview dozens of people—clients and recipients as well as staff and volunteers. The editor's expectation was that my article would show donors how thousands of hours of love poured out by hundreds of volunteers had made an enormous impact on the recipients—and the truth did not disappoint. Redemption shone through in every interview. Hundreds of children, adults, and families experienced long-term life change because a church moved into the neighborhood and chose to be proximal in a relational sense, not merely sharing a zip code.

But that was not all my interviews brought to light. Over and over I found that the volunteers who invested in relationships with their neighbors found *themselves* to be on the receiving end, themselves the ones in need of a neighbor and friend. Unbeknownst to them, *they* were the ones needing to be loved, impacted, helped, and healed, just as much as the people they had come to serve. The volunteers' worldviews, hearts, families, and futures were shaped, redeemed, and changed forever by living in relationship with their "under-resourced" neighbors— who willingly, joyfully, and generously poured themselves out, again and again, opening up their arms and enveloping the volunteers into new homes and families; teaching them insights about God; feeding their bodies, minds, and spirits; and carrying them during times of crisis. Neighbors held babies and brought dinner and taught loyalty and laughter. The change that took place in this community was alchemical—taking two ingredients and transforming them into something entirely new. The magic had an effect on everyone, English speakers and English learners, financially stable and financially vulnerable. Each needed the other. And each had plenty to offer the other. Together, they filled in all the gaps. The giving was never a one-way street.

This is the kind of reciprocal, joy-filled relationship most of us long to have with one another. But as we seek to pivot from isolation to service, we must do so with an awareness of our own vulnerabilities. Those of us with an abundance of material resources often feel a sense of superiority over those who live differently, even though we may not consciously realize it. Rather than seeking a true relationship based on mutuality and trust, we often give charity with an unconscious assumption that "they" are in need and "we" are not, that we have something they lack. Our motivations may be pure, but the result is condescension. There is no faster way to destroy a community—not to mention a relationship—than deadly self-righteousness.

Healthy relationships always go both ways. In healthy relationships, we do not serve our communities because others need the charity we are good enough to provide. When we reach out our hands and hearts in friendship, we ourselves take a risk. We open ourselves up to give *and* receive, acting not out of benevolent superiority but out of neighborliness.

A few years ago, we invited our neighbors over for Thanksgiving. Though they had lived in the US for over ten years, like most newcomers to our country, they had never, not once, been invited to eat a Thanksgiving dinner. They poked each other gleefully, chuckling at our traditions, decorations, and food. A whole bird! Little statues of people dressed up in odd clothing! They nibbled at the food politely. Squash in a pie? Seeing our traditions through their eyes brought a whole new level of enjoyment to my extended family. In return, they invited us to celebrate Día de los Reyes, where my family giggled and fidgeted, chuckling at new traditions and foods. Drinks made from rice? Plastic babies in the cake?

The following Thanksgiving, a well-meaning donor deposited dozens of frozen turkeys at the community-service organization my husband leads, a nonprofit ministry serving our neighborhood. The donor's intentions were wonderful; most of us could use a hand with the grocery budget over the holidays, even more so those struggling to make ends meet. But because he lacked knowledge of and relationship with the people he hoped to bless, his execution was far off the mark. Encumbered by so much generosity, my husband and his staff spent days going door to door, attempting to offload these frozen birds. The residents of our neighborhood—many of whom are immigrants and refugees from around the world—were unfamiliar with large, frozen turkeys and simply did not know what to do with them. Most graciously accepted, far too polite to turn down a gift, but this well-intended donation became a burden for everyone involved.

Days later, an unending stream of cornhusk-wrapped tamales started showing up at our door in a neighborly show of reciprocity. Unsure what to do with a turkey, our neighbors turned them into piles and piles of tamales.

Was this donor loving his neighbors? His heart was in the right place. But his story highlights our desperate need for two-way relationships rather than distant charity. We need proximity, a willingness to assimilate a bit into the rhythms and life-experiences of our neighbors, and enough vulnerability to invite them into our own. We will not know how to love others effectively if we do not know *them*. We will not learn them if we structure our lives so that we do not intersect.

And we will not restructure our lives if our posture toward our neighbors is one of fear rather than love.

This is not our land. None of us own this country, this town, this neighborhood. We are not the hosts. We are merely guests; the whole earth is God's. We live on God's land by God's invitation. Our fellow humans are roommates and equals. We treat each other with dignity and kindness because God has made the terms clear: If we live on God's land, this is how we behave. We serve each other because those are the provisions of the lease God drew up.

BACK TO SCHOOL

Few neighborly decisions determine who a family touches or avoids so much as choosing a school. When my family first moved to our community, we were repeatedly warned: Do not send your kids to the public schools. No matter where I was—walking down the street, shopping at the store, chatting with neighbors in the yard or at church—friends and strangers alike boldly commented on the "failing public schools." Homeschool or private school, they wouldn't dream of telling me what to choose. Just not the public schools. None of these well-meaning community members had personal experience with the schools themselves, but . . . *have you seen the test scores?*

Sometimes I found the grace to gently reply that we had, in fact, done our research and considered the school district a notable asset to the community rather than a liability.

True, a quick glance at our benchmarks and measurables might raise an eyebrow or two. Often my young neighbors come to kindergarten fluent in at least one language but with little exposure to English. Many live below the poverty line, in nutrition-scarce households. A decent percentage of students in the district are supported by parents who diligently work day and night to keep a roof over their heads, but for whom buying computers, getting tutoring, or participating in enrichment activities is out of reach. Many of these adults have been working to support their extended family since adolescence and were never afforded the opportunity to attend high school themselves (or, in some cases, finish primary school)—adding a formal-education gap to the language barrier.

So, the standardized tests tell a scary but incomplete tale. There are so many intangibles these tests are not designed to measure at all: the grit and resiliency and hard work of the families who make up the school community, the strong values and layers of generational support poured into each and every child—to name just a few.

Yet these strengths shine boldly and beautifully. In kindergarten, my daughter was given a large sheet of paper cut into the outline of a house and assigned to paste a colored shape inside the house to represent each type of family member she lived with. A mother would be purple, a father would be green, a sister red, a brother blue, a grandma pink . . . and so on. My child's paper had just a few colors, but her classmates' showed the full rainbow, representing generations of extended family coming together to lend their hard work, loving presence, and energy to the entire family.

Our resilient, resourceful neighborhood schools provide children the opportunity to learn about language and culture, opportunity and empathy, the richness (and complication) that comes with diversity, and the responsibility (and temptation) that comes with privilege. Rubbing elbows each day with friends from radically different histories, children develop self-awareness, others-awareness, empathy, and admiration. They know the world does not all look like they do, or speak the language they do. They know how to befriend and understand someone whose life is different from their own. They know through personal experience the strength of diversity. I love that my children—and their classmates—learn these things each day, along with reading, writing, and arithmetic.

What do we really want when we assess neighborhood schools: a good education, or a school full of children who look and live like we do? Does our concern about test scores extend to our neighbors and their children? How can we seek the peace and prosperity of our city if we are afraid of it?

The trouble with my well-meaning neighbors who warn me against the public schools is that they have little-to-no experience with the schools themselves. They speak confidently of something they don't understand, igniting fear and causing harm to real people in the community. But in truth, some neighborhoods *are* dangerous; some schools do fail their students. I don't want that for my family—or for *any* family. But it is not enough to dodge the bullet ourselves. How could we work together to make the community safe and whole for others as well as ourselves? When those with choices and resources walk away from problems to protect themselves, what happens to those left behind, those who lack the privilege of time or money to choose other options?[5]

I don't expect easy answers to these questions, but it becomes clear to me why God asks Christians to identify as "we," not "me." Real, tangible, complicated problems cannot be solved by one person, or even by a handful. The church must cease to imagine ourself as a place where individuals receive services, and realize that we exist to serve; Christians must learn to see our resources not as a shelter for ourselves but tools to love the community. I long for us to expand the conversation beyond *What is the most I can gain for myself and my family?* to *How could we benefit the whole community, and all our families?* I long for us to make our decisions with a Christlike sense of "ours" over "mine," remembering that love seeks not its own, that the greatest commandment is to care for our neighbor as we care for our own families.

CHAPTER 6

JUBILEE

I'M EATING LUNCH with my new neighbor, Rosa. As I sit in her apartment eating chicken-tinga tostadas, she shares her story. Five years ago, she left two daughters behind and traveled to a new country—my country—with the hope of earning enough money to care for their needs. The journey was horrible; some parts of it she cannot talk about. Now that she lives here in my neighborhood, she works longer hours than I have ever worked, doing harder labor than I have ever done, for less money than I have ever earned. Realistically, she does not expect to see her daughters again, but they talk on the phone and text pictures. Because of the money she sends back to them each month, they go to primary school. They live in a safer location and have enough food to eat.

It's easy to skim past stories like these in a book. But take a moment to consider the reality. Imagine sitting at lunch with a mother who trusts you enough to share the pain she has lived through. Consider *being* that mother. I remember my own children at that age and try to imagine a scenario in which I must leave them behind and move not only into a new neighborhood but a new country, convinced this was the best way I could love and provide for them. In all the worst-case scenarios that run through my head, this has never, ever, come to my mind. It is unthinkable.

And yet, the unthinkable is reality for many of us. Each of our neighbors has a unique story, but they carry the same magnitude and weight. Each time we have the privilege to listen, our understanding of the world may be rocked a bit.

HAVES AND HAVE-NOTS

The response much of the country has to my neighbors—many of them immigrants or refugees—is not the sacrificial love God requires of Christians, but fear. Every day I hear accusations that "they" are "taking over" and "taking our jobs" and "taking our way of life." All this "taking" language makes me wonder what we're really afraid of. Do we suspect that God has not provided enough—or that God's provision is running out? Are we peering into the unknowns of a future we can't control, unsure if God is trustworthy? I feel all these fears myself, often and deeply. But our "taking" language reminds me of toddlers struggling to share their blocks and trucks, and frankly, it says a good deal more about our sinful hearts than it says about my neighbors.

Envy is the sin fueling these fears. Envy feeds on comparison in both directions, causing us to turn on those with more *and* those with less. When someone has more resources or better opportunities than we do, envy tells us we received the raw end of the deal. When someone has less than we do—or a terrifying life story we want to avoid—envy teaches us to lock our doors tightly lest "they" pose a threat to our own comfort. Neither leads to resting in God. Both lead to fearing our neighbors.

In his oft-quoted soliloquy on love, the apostle Paul taught the church at Corinth what it looks like to care for each other, including this little nugget: *Love does not envy.* Decades later, Clement of Rome wrote his own letter to the Corinthian church, imploring them once more to renounce envy, so this must have been an ongoing temptation for the Corinthians. These new Christians were a diverse crowd, grouping together slaves with powerful and wealthy city officials, and everyone in between. Endless tension ensued. The rich preferred to bring their own (better) food to shared meals and struggled to seek equal standing with brothers and sisters if that meant letting go of their own material resources and social status. And so, a stratification infiltrated the community intentionally formed in unity under Christ.

Sound familiar?

Envy is not a sin we are taught to recognize and carefully remove these days. If anything, envy is a way of life we are encouraged to pursue, the primary motivator of our society. How would our economy survive if we weren't driven to buy the latest and greatest? Nevertheless, envy is deadly—especially for a Christian community.

It doesn't take scientific research to see that practicing envy blocks our pursuit of love. We can't afford to spend our life's energy wanting what is not ours, wishing others would lose what they have, or terrified that those with less will threaten what *we* have. Envy festers into fear until everyone becomes a threat—especially those suffering or in poverty—rather than neighbors to know, love, and care for. To ease our discomfort, we avert our eyes and conclude something is wrong with "them"—they must be lazy, or criminal, or lacking morals and family values. Surely their suffering is not something that could happen to good people like *us*. They did something wrong, or we did something right.

Envy blocks the door to empathy. We are so afraid of losing our rights and comforts, but what we squander is the ability to mourn and rejoice with our neighbors.

If our hands are clenched, holding tightly to what we have, we will miss the better thing God offers. I can imagine Jesus' voice affectionately saying, "Do not be afraid, little flock, for your Father has been pleased to give you the kingdom."[1] Jesus did not promise his followers wealth or comfort; after all, he was speaking to peasants in an occupied country. These hardworking folks had just as much (or more) trouble, suffering, and insecurity as the hardworking poor in our own nation. Yet it was to them—not to the wealthy and powerful—that Jesus said, "Don't be afraid. Your Father has given you the Kingdom."

If Jesus asked these folks not to focus on what they had or lacked but to live without fear, surely he asks it of us. Those who belong to Christ, Paul writes, have crucified passions like fear and envy; love, joy, peace, patience, kindness, goodness, faithfulness, gentleness, and self-control are born in us instead.

Love and envy are incompatible. Practicing envy powerfully dislodges the foundation of love we have built in Jesus' name.[2]

But—praise God—the opposite is also true: An active practice of servant-hearted love unravels the envy that tangles up our spirits.

LIVING JUBILEE

Jesus was in Nazareth, his hometown. On the Sabbath, he went to the synagogue with his neighbors, folks he had known since boyhood. The day's reading included passages from Isaiah, and the scrolls were taken from their sacred place, set into Jesus' hands as he stood. Unrolling the parchment, Jesus read from the prophets:

> The Spirit of the Lord is on me,
>   because he has anointed me
>   to proclaim good news to the poor.
> He has sent me to proclaim freedom for the prisoners
>   and recovery of sight for the blind,
> to set the oppressed free,
>   to proclaim the year of the Lord's favor.[3]

Jesus rolled up the scroll and handed it back to be put away. Then, with all eyes watching him, Jesus declared, "Today this scripture has been fulfilled in your hearing."

Can you imagine if a reader in *your* worship service claimed to be the fulfillment of God's redemptive plan? What could Jesus mean? His friends and relatives in the synagogue understood: Jesus was claiming to be the embodiment of God's Jubilee.

When God liberated the Hebrews from Egypt and formed them into a new nation, God made clear that this society, *God's* society, would not stand for injustice and oppression. God had set these people free for *freedom*. But that freedom, as Paul would remind his readers thousands of years later, was not to feed their own appetites. They were freed to serve each other, to build a community where everyone could live in freedom. Since we humans notoriously lose sight of God's passion for justice, God installed checkpoints into the social rhythms: every seven days, every seven years, and every seventh-seventh year would be a Sabbath, a time set apart for God. These Sabbaths would be rest periods, a reset, keeping economic and social systems on track for sustainable, long-term justice.

Every seventh day, no work could be done. The people would trust God by ceasing their labor, and in doing so intro-duced some of the world's earliest labor laws. Neither servant nor animal could work on this holy day. God's people could not grow wealthy through oppressing or exploiting others. A day of joy, rest, and trust was provided for everyone—and this was serious business.

Then, every seventh year was a Sabbatical Year, a year set apart to give relief to the poor and worn down. Debts would be cancelled, rest provided from labor, food and resources supplied to those who lacked. The law would be read aloud, reminding the community what God valued and the constant vigilance justice requires. Because debts were cancelled, indentured slaves were freed on this seventh year, breaking generational enslave-ment. Fields and vineyards were left untended and unharvested for their own long-term health, and as a means to redistribute resources to immigrants, laborers, slaves, servants, and animals, who were encouraged to take what grew naturally in the fields as needed.

Finally, most sacred of all, came the Year of Jubilee: the seventh Sabbatical year, the seventh of the sevens. During this once-in-a-lifetime event, a horn would sound, declaring Jubilee. In addition to all the restorative measures observed every seventh year, all land would be restored to its historical line of inheritance.

Imagine what such a society would be like. Without long-term debt, slavery, or even land and property possession, any accumulated injustice sustained a severe blow every seven years. Wealthy landowners could not impoverish lower classes when debts were erased and bonded servants released every seven years. After fifty years, any land lost reverted back to the family line, providing equal footing for all to work and provide for themselves with no one asserting themselves above the rest for long.

Whether these laws were followed is uncertain—as is our own follow-through in "loving our neighbors as we love ourselves." But everyone understood that when God's redemption came, it would come with Jubilee, establishing a society that freed the prisoner and released the oppressed. This is the theological lesson embedded in the Law, echoed by Isaiah and the Prophets, and later confirmed and announced by Jesus: Throughout all Scripture, God commands his people to build and sustain a just society based on freedom from economic and social oppression. God insists we take radical measures to redistribute wealth at regular intervals, insisting we reset our inevitable slide into injustice each week, each seven years, and each seventh-seventh year. Even today, though neither God nor religious leaders write our cultural norms or laws, God's heart and intentions have not changed. God still commands his people to lean toward Jubilee, toward a society free from oppression.

Now we begin to understand what the community of Nazareth heard that day when Jesus read from Isaiah. Centuries after these laws were given, Jesus said, "I have been anointed [a word hinting at the long-awaited Messiah] to bring good news to the poor, freedom for the prisoner, healing for the blind, and release for the oppressed: to proclaim the *year of Jubilee*. I am God's justice, God's society free from oppression. All that God intended is visible right now before you, in me."

Jesus claimed that *he* was the Messiah, the long-awaited one; that he brought deliverance from injustice. As Jesus said elsewhere,[4] he did not come to abolish the law but to fulfill it: in speaking these words, he was making clear that Sabbath and Jubilee laws were still God's intent, and now were made complete, real, and embodied in Jesus. Jesus' followers will live this way not only for one year but until the Kingdom renders no other way possible: no debt, slavery, oppression, or poverty.

This Kingdom is what we Christians signed up for when we decided to follow Jesus. We are God's embodied Jubilee. We may live in occupied territory as the Babylonian exiles did, but our King is Jesus. We cannot follow the path of envy, looking to grasp and hold and gain, or grow comfortable through the misfortunes of others. We give generously, learning to trade a heart of envy for a life of service. This is how we love our neighbors as we love ourselves, how we care for the whole community as we care for our own family. This is how we love God with all our hearts, and strength, and minds; not you or I alone, but we, the church. There is nothing left for us to envy, nothing left to grasp. We let go of comparison, eagerly and openly sharing all we have with our neighbors, ceasing to be upwardly mobile and instead declaring the Year of Jubilee. We reorient our lives around a very particular set of tasks: proclaiming good news to the poor and freedom for the oppressed; toppling the greedy, power-hungry systems of injustice in the world to further God's Kingdom.[5]

This Kingdom stretches across the entire world and all of history, but for us it begins right now and right here with the first task: caring for our neighbors and community as we would care for our own families, declaring God's Jubilee wherever we are.

Christians believe the living God became our neighbor, that he came and made his dwelling among us, bringing the justice and healing of Jubilee right into the neighborhood. The pain and injustice in our world is staggering; the walk across the street can seem insurmountable. But there is no gift more powerful than the offer of genuine friendship.

These words could change the world: *I am honored to be your neighbor.*

BRAVE STEPS

LOVING OUR NEIGHBORS AS WE LOVE OURSELVES is not something we can accomplish in a day—or alone! We'll need to turn our expectations and way of living over to God again, and again, and again, and relearn how to be in the world. Whether you are reading alone or with a group, take some time with these questions, practices, and activities to discern what loving your real neighbors and community might look like.

REFLECT AND DISCUSS

Do you think of following Jesus as something primarily for your heart and mind to believe, or for your body and life to do? Why?

How does reading the pronoun *you* in the Bible as plural change your understanding of the gospel and the Christian life?

Who are the people in your neighborhood? What are the demographics of your city or town, and how does that compare to the people you know best?

What people in your community do you think of as "those people"—too different from you to really understand or embrace?

Jesus said that all God's law could be summarized by loving God with your heart, soul, and strength, and loving your neighbors as yourself. What do you think Jesus meant by this? How do these two commands together fulfill all that God wants from us?

If your church suddenly closed, would your neighborhood feel the absence? If so, how? If not, why not?

In what ways have you viewed your neighbors with fear? How can you begin to view them with love?

PRACTICE

- Be friendly! When you see someone in your neighborhood, smile and say hello.

- Research your city, town, or neighborhood. What is the history? What are the current demographics? What beliefs, factors, and policies have historically informed who lives where? Consider how you or your family fit into this story.

- Gather a group of Christians together and read one of Paul's Epistles out loud to each other. Change the word "you" to "y'all," "all of you," or another phrase that refers to the full group. Consider and discuss how the instructions for a healthy Christian community sound different when read out loud and addressed to the group, not the individual.

- Go for a long walk around the area where you live (grab some neighbors to go with you!). Pray for the community as you walk, and pay attention to what you see.

- Host an open house for your neighbors. You could start a "Messy Monday" group, offer free popsicles from your front yard every Friday afternoon, or post an open invitation for a potluck in a local park. Or, work with the city to hold a block party. Whether you live in the country, small town, suburbs, or city, look for ways to normalize spending informal time as a community.

- Research ways you can serve your community in an official capacity. Does your library, city, or school board have openings? If a formal job doesn't fit into your schedule, look for ways to serve the people and families who live close to you. Or, start a committee in your church to do a "listening tour" and find out where the needs are in your community and how your church's resources of time and energy can help. Remember to seek out mutual relationships and genuine friendship whenever possible.

LOOK AND LISTEN
- *Jesus Calls His Disciples* painting by He Qi
- "Ring the Bells" song by JOHNNYSWIM / Drew Holcomb & the Neighbors

Find this art or music, then spend time sitting with it. What do you see and hear? What invitation is God offering you through them?

SECTION THREE

STRANGERS

Faith is God's call to see his trace in the face of the Other.

JONATHAN SACKS

AN EXPERT IN BIBLICAL LAW AND THEOLOGY approaches Jesus and asks, "What must I do to gain eternal life?"[1] His tone is hostile, testing. He is not a seeker; he already knows the answer. Moreover, Jesus knows that he knows.

"You know the law," Jesus counters. "How do you read it?"

"'Love the Lord your God with all your heart and with all your soul and with all your strength and with all your mind' and, 'Love your neighbor as yourself,'" the expert replies.

"Correct," Jesus confirms. "If you do this, you will live."

Interesting, isn't it? "Do this," Jesus says. Not recite this. Not believe this. *Do* this.

The expert wants to prove himself, so he plows forward: "But who is my neighbor?"

Just a few moments earlier, Jesus declared that the things of God's Kingdom were hidden from the wise and learned but revealed instead to little children. And so, to this tricky wise man, this Bible-trivia winner, Jesus does not argue law but tells a story.

"A man was traveling from this city to that city—a common road but a dangerous road. You wouldn't want to be there alone; you would pass through as quickly and unnoticed as possible. But there was no other way to go from here to there. And so it was with this man. He was attacked, robbed, stripped of everything, even his clothes, and beaten. By the time the robbers were finished they had discarded him in the ditch, nearly dead.

"Then along came a priest, traveling home from a day's work in the holy city, fulfilling his holy duties of worship in the temple. After him came another traveler, also a clergyman, also returning home after a day of holy work at the temple.

Approaching a potentially dead body would mean defilement, triggering complicated cleansing rituals. So, each of them chose to pass by on the other side, safely away.

"Then a third man approached. Unlike the others, he was not close to home, not returning from sacred duties of worship. In fact, this man would have been considered an outcast in the eyes of everyone we have met in the story until now—the robbers, the suffering traveler, the priest and clergyman. Each of them would have considered this man a foreigner, an outcast, and a heretic, one who did not know or worship God correctly: an enemy. Yet this traveler ran up to the man who lay near death, saw a fellow human in need, and began working quickly. Doing what he could to clean the wounds with oil, ease his pain with wine, and stop the bleeding, he lifted the man onto his donkey and brought him to an inn where he could care for him properly, paying for all the expenses himself.

"So," Jesus asks, "who was the neighbor?"

This is a surprising follow-up question. None of the men traveling lived near each other, so none were neighbors at all in that sense. The robbers saw in their fellow traveler an expendable source of resources. The clergymen saw in the man's suffering a demand on their energy that distracted from "true" worship. Only one person looked upon this beaten and dying man, in a dangerous place, at an inconvenient time, and saw not an enemy or an oppressor (though he was both), nor a distraction, expense, or danger (though he was all those things too) but a fellow human in need of mercy.

The one person in the story known to everyone listening as a stranger, an intruder, a heretic, is the one God reveals as the neighbor. The one who did not worship the true God is the one Jesus says truly obeys and loves God—and, to answer the religious expert's question—the one who will inherit eternal life.

CHAPTER 7

STRANGER THINGS

MY PHONE RANG AT 4:00 A.M., which is never a good sign.

I had traveled to Salt Lake City the evening before, an urgent, last-minute attempt to see my grandmother before she died. Walking into the room where my mother had kept vigil for days, I held Grandma's withered hand and placed my head on her chest. "I'm here," I whispered. "I made it in time." She didn't respond, of course; she hadn't responded in days. But I was there. I was holding her hand one last time.

An hour or so later, I made my way to a nearby hotel room, having made plans to return in the early morning—unless my mother called me sooner. Sure enough, after a few hours of sleep, my phone rang.

At 4:20 a.m., a car with an Uber sticker on the windshield arrived to pick me up. The driver was the first person I'd spoken to since hearing the news, and I couldn't stop myself. "Thanks for picking me up," I greeted this stranger as I stepped into his car. "My grandma just died. You're taking me to see her. I'm here to help my mom."

Talk about oversharing. This complete stranger, who surely wished he were sleeping or at least driving a quieter passenger, looked me straight in the eyes through his rearview mirror and said, "The next few hours and days will be hard. But you can do this. You are strong enough to do this. You will make it through this day." For the rest of the drive, he alternated between words of encouragement and praying for my family. As I stepped out of the car, I looked him in the eyes once more and thanked him sincerely. "You have been a minister of grace to me today," I said.

Later in the day, after the whirlwind had subsided, I thought of the proverbial Good Samaritan in Jesus' story. I was a traveler, unexpectedly finding myself in a moment of need. A stranger learned of my situation (albeit through the Uber app) and cared for me like family.

As we have seen, Jesus invites—commands—his followers to live out of a posture of love rather than fear, out of a love which *conquers* fear. We who follow Jesus are asked to extend the care we provide our own families to our neighbors and communities. But how far does this command extend? Certainly, this includes those living nearby, the people whose shoulders rub our own. But Jesus made it abundantly clear that anyone we meet who is in need falls under this umbrella—no matter where they live, no matter what their religion, race, or creed. Christians are those who encounter strangers and see neighbors, family. We *become* the neighbors, the hands and feet of Jesus, wherever we go, whatever it costs us.

That's a big ask. That's the sort of task that could consume a person's whole life. But then again, Jesus said it would. He said it would be hard, that it would require everything. He certainly didn't say it would be safe.

THE BUTTER BATTLE

In his children's story *The Butter Battle Book*, Dr. Seuss tells of the Yooks and the Zooks, two ethnic groups (if that's the right description for these furry creatures) who live next to each other. One society wears only blue clothing, the other only orange. Most importantly, the Yooks eat their bread with the butter side up, while the Zooks eat their bread with the butter side down. This fundamental difference in two otherwise identical factions leads first to suspicion: There must be something wrong with *them* if they choose to live *that* way, when *our* way is so clearly good and right. Suspicions grow into certainty, until suddenly, instead of neighbors, the two tribes are outright enemies, devising more and more effective ways to destroy each other.

Dr. Seuss wrote this book in the 1980s as a cautionary tale against the Cold War, and I've found it a useful summary of human nature in general. Whether *they* live on the other side of the tracks or the other side of the border, we tend to focus on differences and eye *those people* with suspicion. Why do they live like that instead of like this? Is something *wrong* with them?

When we believe the worst about each other, we do the worst *to* each other out of misplaced self-preservation, and it's all downhill from there. As Dr. Seuss demonstrated in *The Butter Battle Book*, we rarely know where the fears and hatreds we nurture each day originated—or where they will lead.

When Jesus was asked how to inherit eternal life, he tossed the question back to the expert of God's law. Jesus did not offer a new answer. Jewish law and tradition already held the key, as easy to rattle off as your own first name: Love God with all your heart and soul and strength, and love your neighbor as yourself. When the expert tested Jesus, looking for more specifics by clarifying, "But who is my neighbor?" Jesus told an incredibly provocative story. In Jesus' story, the "real" religious people, who believed the right things and knew the right answers and led the people in worship, were not the ones *doing the work* of loving God and loving their neighbor. But Jesus' insult did not stop there: It was a Samaritan, an outsider, who demonstrated true love of God and neighbor.

To the man asking, and the crowd listening, Samaritans were ancient relatives who had become foreigners, neighbors who had become enemies. Since the Babylonian exile, Jews and Samaritans had lived in ever-increasing hostility, with acts of harassment, prejudice, and open aggression on both sides. The Jews would add hours to their travels rather than so much as pass through Samaria. They certainly would not consider a Samaritan a potential ally—much less an example of godly living or the recipient of eternal life.

So when Jesus drove his story home by saying, "It is the foreigner, the heretic, the enemy of yours caring for a suffering stranger who pleases God, not the people you consider godly and righteous"—these were fighting words. It would be as if Jesus appeared today and announced that Muslim refugees or Latin American migrant caravans were more in step with God's plan than American pastors and podcasters. As if he told the

Yooks and Zooks that serving each other, not how you butter your bread, is what counts.

How do we even begin to grapple with this idea Jesus lays out? Are we ready to follow a savior, and worship a God, who is more interested in our compassion than our safety, more invested in how we care for strangers than how we police our theological (and national) borders?

KEEPING VIGIL

Introvert that I am, I have a hard time knocking on doors even when I've been invited, harder still if I don't know anyone on the other side. But one day I accepted an invitation from a complete stranger to come to dinner. My hosts, whom I met for the first time that night, were recent refugees from Syria, a land suffering from years of civil war. Just weeks after arriving in this strange new country, they received word that several members of their family back in Syria had been killed in a bombing.

Facing the deepest grief of their lives during a time of personal upheaval, the family had no way to return home to grieve with their community and absolutely no community in this new country to grieve with. So they invited strangers. Several of us from the neighborhood and from church came that night, sitting in metal folding chairs pushed against the wall as men and women we didn't know served us plate after plate of their favorite Syrian dishes. This family had lost everything dear to them, and the best way they knew to process their grief was to cook for strangers.

It is hard for me to understand what good it did for me to sit on that chair and eat plates heaped with food. Our hosts spoke only Arabic. We guests spoke English or Spanish. I used hand gestures to communicate my sympathy, but mostly I sat there for a long time, eating and sitting, sitting and eating. The family's three-year-old daughter eventually climbed up on my pastor's lap and stayed there for hours.

Though we had no language in common, we were fellow humans. We all know what it feels like to be afraid, to lose more love than we can live without. These strangers needed people to sit in their living room, so we came and sat. It was a never-to-be-forgotten honor.

In an essay exploring how the early church understood Jesus' teaching, Gerhard Lohfink considers the biblical command to "love your neighbor as yourself," the same command Jesus explored in the parable of the Good Samaritan. Lohfink concluded that the listeners of ancient Israel would have understood it this way:

> "Love your neighbor as yourself" means: The help and solidarity that everyone in Israel owes his own relatives, especially his direct family, should be extended to all Israelites. The boundaries of one's own family should be broken through so as to include the whole people of God as brothers and sisters—including strangers, and even those whom one's family and relatives consider enemies. That is what Leviticus 19 is saying.[1]

Lohfink goes on to say that in telling this story the way he does, Jesus clarifies that the practice of caring for all fellow humans as neighbors—including strangers, even enemies—is inherently connected to loving God, one and the same thing.

The question of how we treat strangers is such a hot topic for social and political debate in our world today that it might be hard for us to remember who's talking in this story: This is not a pundit or a reporter, not a conservative or a liberal. This is Jesus, the Son of God, from the right hand of the Father. Those of us who follow Jesus must take this seriously, regardless of the current political climate—and we cannot do it alone. The body of Christ is meant to be the community that cares for everyone inside the community—and everyone outside the community—as though they were our own family.

But is this commitment to loving strangers what we are known for?

In reality, many Christians in the United States are more likely to fear strangers than love them. In a recent study, PRRI reported that over 50 percent of white evangelical Christians considered immigrants a threat to their values and security, a far higher percentage than any other religious affiliation, and nearly twenty points higher than the population as a whole.[2] When asked to describe their beliefs about immigrants, nearly half of evangelicals saw recent immigrants as an undesirable drain on economic resources. The majority of Americans in every demographic support welcoming refugees (a different legal classification from immigrants) into the United States— *except* for white evangelical Christians. Instead, the majority of white evangelicals favor preventing refugee resettlement in the USA.[3] When asked what one factor influenced their thinking on these matters, only 12 percent of evangelicals cited Jesus or the Bible and only 2 percent cited their local church community or teaching. Only one in five evangelicals reported that their local church had encouraged them to reach out to immigrants in their community at all; the rest had never heard such a thing mentioned at church.[4]

I wonder: If we asked Jesus how to gain eternal life, what parable would he tell us today?

WHO IS MY STRANGER?

Jesus' words to the legal expert seeking eternal life are packed with meaning for us two thousand years later, meaning that intends to upend our lives and communities for the better—though upsetting power structures and getting us into trouble in the process. But Jesus was not teaching a new idea. The Jewish law and prophets already made God's expectation for society abundantly clear. That's why the expert knew the answer, even if he (like myself, to be honest) preferred not to apply it too closely in his real life.

Sometime after the expert asked his question, Jesus told another parable, which we call the parable of the tenants. In this story, a vineyard owner sends messengers to collect the harvest from the tenants—but the tenants beat the messengers and throw them out. This happens more than once. Finally, the owner sends his own son, assuming that the heir will be given respect. But the tenants kill him.

In telling this story, Jesus provokes anger by insinuating that he is the proverbial son. After the prophets were ignored and mistreated by those in power, Jesus the Son came to clarify what God had already and clearly and repeatedly said he wanted—even if we hated his message so much that we killed him.

And we did. I imagine we would again, if he came to us today. We are all too willing to leave the people God commands us to love along the side of the road. We've learned to respond not out of love but out of fear.

In the Hebrew Scriptures, the word *stranger*—also translated *sojourner, foreigner,* or *alien*—appears almost fifty times in the Pentateuch, and refers specifically to a "resident alien," someone from another country who has come to live among us. God reminds Israel again and again that they are a nation of immigrants. At God's command Abraham left his home behind and became a sojourner. Jacob's family traveled to Egypt for financial assistance during severe famine, living for generations as perpetual outsiders until their offspring were enslaved for still more generations. Once liberated and formed into a new nation, they continued to sojourn through the wilderness, seeking a homeland. God made clear that injustices like they experienced must never become part of how they treat others. Once the Hebrews had their own land, they must treat the foreigners and strangers among them with dignity and care—the opposite of how they were treated in Egypt. And so, laws outlining justice, compassion, and protection were extended to strangers. In fact, the law and the prophets make clear that *special* regard and dignity should be shown to immigrants and travelers:

> The alien who resides with you shall be to you as the
> citizen among you; you shall love the alien as yourself,

for you were aliens in the land of Egypt: I am the LORD your God.[5]

[Moses said,] "Cursed is anyone who withholds justice from the foreigner, the fatherless or the widow."
    Then all the people shall say, "Amen!"[6]

Thus says the LORD of hosts: Render true judgments, show kindness and mercy to one another; do not oppress the widow, the orphan, the alien, or the poor; and do not devise evil in your hearts against one another.[7]

You shall allot it as an inheritance for yourselves and for the aliens who reside among you and have begotten children among you. They shall be to you as citizens of Israel; with you they shall be allotted an inheritance among the tribes of Israel.[8]

If you truly amend your ways and your doings, if you truly act justly one with another, if you do not oppress the alien, the orphan, and the widow, or shed innocent blood in this place, and if you do not go after other gods to your own hurt, then I will dwell with you in this place, in the land that I gave of old to your ancestors forever and ever.[9]

These powerful words are only a few of the commandments about immigrants and travelers, and they reflect God's heart and plan for humanity. But in the centuries between Moses and the kings, society became so twisted that the prophets were called upon to remind powerful citizens that God seeks justice and a community that cares deeply even for strangers. This message was forgotten again between the prophets and Jesus, forgotten so entirely that Jesus' confrontational reminders were threatening enough to make the religious leaders seek to silence him through death.

What are the chances, then, that we and our religious systems, our social ethics, our morality, and our understanding of God's salvation have once more gone down the slippery slope of forgetting that Jesus said eternal life is found by loving God and our neighbor—and that our neighbor means anyone we encounter in need, whether we know them or not, whether we think they would side with us or against us?

Jesus' teaching is not a philosophy or a theory, not something we can merely agree with. Some years after Jesus' death and resurrection, the author of 1 John began his letter by saying, "That which was from the beginning, which we have heard, which we have seen with our eyes, which we have looked at and our hands have touched—this we proclaim concerning the Word of life."[10] In other words, this stuff is *real*, and it informs how we live our real life. We have seen it, touched it, looked it over, held it in our hands. The good news happens—or doesn't happen—in our very real bodies, in how we use our bodies, how we treat other bodies—be they family, neighbor, or stranger.

STRANGER DANGER

Here we are again at the dilemma that haunts us: fear. Caring for strangers in need—whether they are for or against us—won't always be in our best interest. It certainly wasn't in the best interest of the two clergymen who passed by the dying man. The Good Samaritan wasn't safe on that dangerous road between Jerusalem and Jericho; he didn't give out of the abundance of his privilege but out of basic human dignity. Jesus wasn't safe in anything he did or said, and neither were his followers—not before his death and resurrection, and even less so afterward. Yet they realized that revering God went hand in hand with honoring *all* humans in need, no matter how dangerous, strange, or uncompelling they may be to us.

Not many years ago, an African American prayer group welcomed a strange white man to their prayer meeting. After studying the Bible and praying side by side with them for nearly an hour, the stranger opened fire and massacred them.[11] Statements made by the killer, and later by the three surviving church members, demonstrate that while loving strangers may very well open doors to danger, closing doors in hatred leads to certain violence. It was not the love and welcome of the victims that resulted in their murders—but the toxic fears of the murderer.[12]

Jesus' commands are not naive to reality. Strangers may turn out to be enemies. Our fears are deeply entrenched, often for good reason. Jesus himself was brutally killed by neighbors and strangers, and many of his followers were as well. Still, our calling as Christians is this: If we follow Jesus on the path to eternal life, we will choose the love that conquers fear and hate.

Following Jesus is not about disregarding danger. Jesus warned his followers to count the cost, to imagine picking up a cross and heading toward rejection, suffering, possible death.

Let's not downplay the consequences. But also, let's not downplay the rewards. We don't choose to live in God's Kingdom because it's safe, but because we're compelled by God's beautiful plan to make all things new. A woman doesn't give birth because it's safe and easy. There's a risk to her life at every step of the process—but also the hope of new life. Young adults don't become firefighters or first responders looking for a safe profession. They wake up each morning knowing their lives might be on the line—but they will save lives in the process. We don't choose to follow Jesus because it's the safest option either, but because we have experienced God's love and been transformed. We have seen a glimpse of the Kingdom right here in our communities and found it worth working for. We have heard the beautiful song of redemption, and there is no turning us back.

CHAPTER 8

BECOMING ANGELS

I SAT IN THE DRIVER'S SEAT, pushing the gas pedal all the way to the floor—and going nowhere. My husband, Matthew, was two cars behind me, standing with his back against our house's foundation and pushing with all his might. It was a bizarre situation, to say the least.

Earlier that morning, we had rented a truck from the hardware store to haul our new bedroom furniture home. Since our house does not have a garage or driveway, we backed the truck as close to the front door as we could. But in the January mix of snow, ice, and mud, the truck slid toward the house until the foundation flagstones stopped its progress. Our attempts to drive the truck out of the yard resulted only in losing ground as the tires spun deeper into the mud. We were doubly stuck, paying by the minute for the past-due rental truck that refused to budge.

After trying nearly every trick we could think of, Matthew attached the truck to our own car with the strongest ropes we owned. He pushed the truck from behind while I attempted to tow the truck out with our car—to absolutely no avail. What we needed was a set of chains and a more powerful towing vehicle. But none of our neighbors were home on this wintery morning, and the tow truck we called estimated a two-hour wait. We could hear the dollars trickling out of our bank account as the minutes ticked by.

We live on a busy road, the main drag going through town. Our jumble of jimmy-rigged towing vehicles jutted far into the street. At least ten cars per minute approached us, slowed, gawked, and then inched around us—without stopping. This had been going on for over an hour, my husband and I clearly struggling and failing, while hundreds of our neighbors passed by on the other side.

Many of the vehicles passing were pickup trucks, well-appointed for solving our problem. I started making eye contact with the drivers, a pleading and exasperated look on my face. The only result was that the drivers stopped gawking, avoiding making eye contact with me entirely as they slid around us and went on their way. Slamming my fist down on the steering wheel, I shouted, "What is *wrong* with our *neighbors?*"

Finally, *finally*, a driver stopped. Pulling his truck up to our house, he got out of his car and walked over as Matthew and I danced a jig of relief. We were saved! The man, we learned, had recently moved to our country and did not speak much English. But our problem was obvious; a few hand gestures did the trick. With his four-wheel drive and chains, our rental truck was unstuck in two minutes. Matthew and I shook hands with this Good Samaritan and asked if we could pay him for his trouble. "No, no," he insisted. With more hand signals and a smile, he made clear that someday he would be the one in need of a neighbor.

Once the now-incredibly-expensive-but-thankfully-unharmed rental truck had been returned to the hardware store, Matthew and I surveyed the damage to our lawn and siding, reflecting on the strange encounter. How fitting, we agreed, that after hundreds of our own community members drove by, watching us struggle but passing by on the other side of the street, it was a stranger, a sojourner who stopped to help us, who recognized that simply being in need rendered us holy, worthy—a neighbor.

HOSPITALITY

When I imagine the gift of hospitality, my thoughts go immediately to a few friends of mine. Visits to their homes feel like mini vacations, with every detail planned exactly with you in mind. You'll have tea on the porch, or brunch in the yard with candles hanging from the ancient willow overhead. The decor will be perfectly themed for the season, with everything comfortably arranged, your every whim predicted and accounted for. The host or hostess will be calm and disarming, fully present and enjoying the experience they have artfully created. From the time you arrive until the minute you leave, each guest is honored. The experience is delightful.

Receiving this gift is like receiving a sacrament. For a moment you cannot help but be convinced how valuable and lovely you are. The women and men who can surround another person in this cloud of grace astound me.

Also: Words cannot properly express how entirely *I do not have this gift*. I can hardly pull off a hot dinner for my family, much less welcome guests with place settings, centerpieces, and soothing music. You're more than welcome to come, and I hope that you do; but keep your expectations low (and maybe bring a pizza).

There is both good news and bad news for people like me, and the good news comes first: This miraculous gift that we call hospitality is not strictly the biblical concept of hospitality. Wonderful and beneficial though these lovely meals certainly are, the Christian practice of hospitality doesn't entail hosting fancy dinners but caring for strangers, whether they come to the door or we encounter them in the street.

The (not really) bad news is that as a follower of Christ, I am commanded to practice this, whether it falls into my gifting or not. Romans 12 says, "Don't just pretend to love others. Really love them. . . . When God's people are in need, be ready to help them. Always be eager to practice hospitality."[1] Or, as 1 Peter 4 implores us, "Cheerfully share your home with those who need a meal or a place to stay."[2] Hebrews 13 reminds us to "keep on loving one another as brothers and sisters. Do not forget to show hospitality to strangers, for by so doing some people have shown hospitality to angels without knowing it."[3] The Bible is clear and consistent about the need to offer our resources of food, shelter, and fellowship with those—friend and stranger—who need it.

In her book *Making Room: Recovering Hospitality as a*

Christian Tradition, Christine D. Pohl reminds us of the biblical assumption, long lost to our cultural mind-set, that Christians will extend hospitality to strangers, both fellow Christians and anyone in need, as a central piece of the gospel. She says, of her own experience on the receiving end, "It was there that I first saw how much more powerfully the gospel spoke when those who were teaching opened their homes and their lives to strangers—with no pretense, no perfection, but extraordinary faithfulness and generosity. Their hospitality made the Christian life both credible and inviting to many who stayed with them."[4]

Biblically speaking, Christians can expect a warm meal and bed with newly met brothers and sisters, no matter where they travel. Biblically, it's reasonable to hope that the needs in our communities, from hunger to homelessness to loneliness, will be eased by our commitment to hospitality—whether or not we have "the gift."

STRANGERS SEEKING SHELTER

My daughter and I were enjoying a lovely summer sunset on the porch when an evening stroll struck our fancy. We stepped off the porch and headed down the sidewalk under a blue sky. Just a few moments later, however, the sky began to turn. I recall saying, "I think it's going to storm. We probably shouldn't go too far" before we had gotten to the end of our block. Before we turned the corner, the sky was completely dark. I've never seen weather change so rapidly. We turned around quickly, running for home—but already tree branches were falling around us, the wind roaring with the train-like sound of an approaching tornado. Though we were just down the street from home, I began looking for lights on in the houses we ran past.

We made it home safely, looking out from the protection of our window at the street already lined in fallen tree branches, wondering how the sky had gone from lovely to deadly in just a few minutes. I told my daughter that I almost ran into a stranger's house instead of trying to make it home. She was dumbstruck: Running into the house of a stranger is *not* allowed. Yes—but if the alternative was being hit by a tree or swept up in a funnel cloud, I was willing to risk impropriety.

In ancient times, nearly every culture had sacred traditions and laws about hosting strangers, some of which remain today; most of us feel confident our fellow humans would extend compassion and care if it were desperately needed. There was good reason for this practice back then: If you were traveling before electricity, gasoline engines, and Holiday Inn, you had to think quickly when the sun went down. It might be safe to pitch a tent and light a fire along the road, but extreme temperatures, wild animals, and robbers made camping in the open incredibly risky. Plus, you could only carry so much food and water in your bags, and then what? There was no 7-Eleven or McDonald's along the route.

Being away from shelter and community wasn't safe. So, if a stranger came to your door in need of food, water, or shelter, you gave it. To decline—while certainly the safer and more comfortable option for you and your family—might directly result in the death of your would-be guest. And almost certainly, you and your loved ones would find yourself in a similar position one day, depending on strangers to uphold their end of this sacred calling.

In ancient Greece, this universal calling to human decency was called *xenia*, or guest-friendship, a sacred obligation all people had to those traveling far from home. So hallowed was this duty that the Greeks believed the gods would perform quality-control spot checks, showing up disguised as a poor or sickly person to see if the homeowner would provide shelter and supplies.[5] These stories acted as incentives, for there was a chance the stranger at your door might secretly be an angel or a god, and a reward or punishment might depend on your decision.

Xenia makes sense of one of the final stories Jesus told before his death. Asking the crowd to imagine the King on his throne, coming to judge all humanity, Jesus says that people will be separated into two groups as a shepherd separates sheep and goats. One group the King banishes from his sight, sending them away to eternal punishment; the other he invites to himself, offering the reward of eternal life. When members of each group questioned how they came to be sorted as they were, the King replied that his decision was based on who had offered him food when he was hungry, drink when he was thirsty, clothes when he lacked them, care when he was sick or in prison, and shelter when he was a stranger.

Still both groups were baffled. When had they ever seen their Lord and King in such need and withheld—or offered—these things? The King replied, "Whatever you did for the least of my brothers and sisters you did for me."[6] In other words, the poor, sick, hungry, thirsty person you saw? That was the King in disguise all along. Not just once or twice for a spot check but each and every time. Jesus tells this story to clarify that anytime we see a human in need, God expects us to assume this person is *him*, who created the world and liberated his people from bondage, who took on flesh and made himself a servant—and behave accordingly.

In his story, Jesus drives home all the law and prophets, the greatest commandments, the sum of the Bible and the gospel, the full meaning of the parable of the Good Samaritan: Our love for God is measured on whether we show hospitality to strangers, to whomever needs it, whomever they may be.

Once again, Jesus takes this command seriously, putting eternal life and punishment on the line. I suspect this feels strange to most of us, for this way of thinking and practicing our faith simply isn't what most Christians are taught in America. Imagine receiving a tract outlining ways to care for strangers, reminding you that your eternity was at stake. Or an altar call where the pastor pleads with you to turn your resources over to those in need, begging you to heed the words of Jesus regarding the destination of your soul! I have never heard even a hint of such a thing. Yet over and over, Jesus told his followers—especially the religious ones—that the way to eternal life is through following him, through caring for neighbors and strangers with the care and hospitality we give to our own families. If this was true when Jesus walked the earth, why wouldn't it still be true today?

Let us stop to consider an even graver reality: In our churches and Christian conversations, we are often encouraged to do the opposite of what Jesus calls us to do. In her book *The Myth of the American Dream*, D. L. Mayfield says of her Christian upbringing, "We did not feel a sense of responsibility to the wider world and in fact were encouraged to shun it."[7]

Did this message seep into your upbringing and soul as well? The idea, even subtle, perhaps unspoken, that people outside the Christian circle—especially strangers—are dangerous? They might hurt our communities, or weaken our values, or upset the balance of society. They might prove to be a temptation, create a slippery slope. Best to keep as much distance as possible. In so many ways we have been discipled to join the priest and the Levite, taught to carefully cross the street on the other side lest our holiness be tarnished or our safety threatened by those who most need compassion.

Daily, if not hourly, I hear messages from friends, teachers, preachers, authors, and media warning that strangers and foreigners are traveling into our country, entering our cities and neighborhoods. I hear it around the family holiday table and the television in the salon waiting room. I hear it used to sell books (*Beware!*) and products (*Be safe!*) and even to convert us to Christianity (*Be on your guard!*). But the warning siren is not imploring us to step up and welcome these immigrants, refugees, and asylum seekers as our sacred Christian duty. No: We are warned that these strangers are threatening our way of life and livelihood by bringing disease,[8] stealing our jobs, and eroding our values.

I imagine Jesus weeping over us, as he once wept over Jerusalem, for we have removed ourselves from the peace he offers.[9] We should weep, too, for if we view the Christian life as *not* requiring our active, compassionate care of strangers in need of food, water, shelter, and community, then the Christian way of life has already shriveled up and died. The Christian way of life—the life of following Jesus—extends compassionate love and actively provides care to anyone in need, treating them with the same honor and dignity we would muster if that person were *God*. If we, ourselves, have removed this radical hospitality from our understanding and exercise of our faith, what danger could the secular world pose to us? We have abandoned the practice of Christianity; there is nothing left for these strangers to steal.

God's calling—indeed, God's invitation and command—is for us to be a blessing. Not to hoard resources for ourselves, not to keep ourselves safe like talents buried in the ground,[10] but to pour ourselves out. To care for those in need. To seek the peace of the city.

ENTERTAINING ANGELS

Sodom and Gomorrah were twin cities so full of evil that God saw it best to destroy them entirely. This ancient saga is recounted in Genesis but referenced many times throughout the Bible and still today. Truly, it is a grisly tale. We use it to warn against what we assume were these folks' primary manifestations of evil: heinous sexual sin, including both heterosexual and homosexual rape.

But ask a reader from a more traditional or collectivist culture and you get an additional answer that's hidden from Western eyes: The cities' sin was their lack of hospitality, their failure to treat strangers and foreigners in a way that elevates their dignity and prioritizes their protection. To my surprise, both the prophets and Jesus read the story this way too. The prophet Ezekiel said, "Now this was the sin of your sister Sodom: She and her daughters were arrogant, overfed and unconcerned; they did not help the poor and needy. They were haughty and did detestable things before me."[11] Both Matthew and Luke record Jesus describing the towns that failed to welcome his traveling disciples: "I tell you, it will be more bearable on that day for Sodom than for that town."[12]

The violent and nonconsensual sexual atrocities committed by the people of Sodom and Gomorrah were clearly evil—both in the story as well as in our own consciences. But I'm struck by the fact that non-Westerners (including Jesus!) read this story *primarily* as an indictment of their lack of hospitality, which was considered at least as evil as these unspeakable acts. To put it bluntly: Today we would never consider lack of hospitality on par with gang rape. How significantly would our perspectives toward our fellow humans, our sense of responsibility to strangers, and our understanding of God's will need to change for that to happen? How would our Christian communities and personal choices be reshaped in light of God's strong language around these issues?

Centuries after the events in Genesis, the writer of Hebrews warns readers to always offer hospitality to strangers, knowing they may well be hosting angels. And, as Tremper Longman points out in his teaching on this story,[13] the people of Sodom did, indeed, entertain angels that day. In 1 Timothy, Paul includes this habit of hospitality among the traits necessary for church leadership[14]—which we somehow fail to prioritize as highly as other characteristics mentioned in that passage.

But even when we are not accommodating angelic beings, our fellow humans bear the image of God. In the Creator's eyes, each person carries the weight of glory[15] and deserves the dignity and honor befitting the *imago Dei*—every single person.

EUCHARIST

There is one meal where Christians regularly gather, receiving and sharing with all who come: the Eucharist, or the Lord's Supper. In this sacrament, this sacred moment of grace, Christians all around the world come to the table from every race, class, language, ethnicity, tradition, and country of origin and share a meal together in unity and equality, every one of us under Jesus—even if we are not in the same physical space or time. But how do we live when we get up from the table? Do we extend the grace of this meal to every part of our lives? Or do we shrink back, going into our regular lives fearing and attacking those with whom we shared the bread and the wine?

The early church, living under the Roman Empire, faced the same question. Men and women of wealth and power gathered with slaves and peasants, sitting together as equals at Christ's table. But what then? It took effort and sacrifice to care for each other in the day-to-day world, but they took the commands seriously.

They weren't perfect at it. They were humans struggling with sin and selfishness just as we are. These Christians lived inside a cultural system that penalized crossing political, economic, and class lines even more than our culture does. Many of Paul's letters contain coaching along these lines—what it looks like to let go of one's own rights and freedom and place in society to care for each other—which tells me that the old ways died hard.

They weren't immune to abusing the system, either. Early Christian writings include a caveat for strangers settling into a new place: After two or three days, skilled workers and able-bodied travelers must begin working for their provisions and not "live in idleness simply on the strength of being a Christian" and so "exploit Christ."[16] These failures and temptations would not be mentioned so often if giving and receiving healthy hospitality came easily.

Yet we have also seen how the Emperor Julian complained that the followers of Jesus made his own people look bad by outdoing them in caring for each other *and* for the strangers outside their ranks.

To be honest, I can't imagine what it would look like in our time and place if Christians took Jesus at his word and considered strangers with dignity, love, and sacred compassion rather than fear. We do live in a world full of 7-Elevens and Holiday Inns, so I doubt there would be many knocks on the door from people truly in a bind for food, water, and shelter. More likely, I envision a free-for-all for scammers and charlatans, for we humans tend to corrupt any system. But we can change the way we talk about strangers, whether sojourners passing through, immigrants moving into town, migrants seeking aid at our borders, or neighbors of different beliefs and backgrounds. We can change our posture and attitude at the very least and be ready to welcome and care for and give sacrificially at a moment's notice. If the Christian church were to treat strangers and foreigners with the dignity that we ascribe to Christ—and do so seriously, with the weight of eternity—the world would be a vastly different place.

In Jesus' warning is an invitation for us. While caring for strangers we may unknowingly care for an angel. But even if we don't, we will *become* angels—messengers of God—the hands and feet of Jesus in ways we'll never expect and may never know.

CHAPTER 9

THE STRANGE IMAGE OF GOD

IN ONE OF MY FIRST MEMORIES, I am five years old, picking my way down rows of steep bleacher seats, grasping my mother's hand. My other hand clutches a rare treat: my very own box of Milk Duds. Contrary to the popular expression, this *is* my first rodeo. I look across the vast sea of humanity filling the massive stadium. (Okay, it was a few hundred folks sitting on wooden bleachers at our small county fair, but at age five it *felt* massive.)

I wasn't excited or even curious: I was terrified.

It wasn't the crowd that bothered me that day, or the rickety steps or the height of the seats. As I took in the sights and sounds—the audience, the costumed performers, the animals waiting below—my brain went straight to the Roman Colosseum. I had learned recently of the slaves forced to fight to the death, of the Christians compelled to renounce their faith or be thrown to the lions. The story was used not only to teach me history but to warn me: This could happen again. I didn't have the cultural acumen to understand how ancient Rome differed from rural Wisconsin, so as I took in the elliptical stadium circling a dirt floor filled with aggressive-looking animals, the pieces fell into place.

Then, disaster struck. As I bit down on the stale caramel center of a Milk Dud, my first loose tooth wiggled free. My mouth was bleeding, so my mother gathered me up for a trip to the bathroom, and I could no longer contain my fears. We *would not* leave my dad here, alone in the stands. *Could not, would not.* What if he was taken while we were gone?

My sweet, nurturing parents, ignorant of my terror—and really, who could possibly have anticipated it?—watched my breakdown with utter bewilderment.

You won't be surprised to learn we made it home safely that night; aside from the tooth incident, the day was drama-free. I may have been terrified of the strangers surrounding me, but there was no actual threat to my family's safety. It turns out a rodeo in Wisconsin is not a place where Christians are thrown to the lions.

The actual Colosseum? Well, that's another story.

Practicing the new Christian religion in the first two centuries was technically illegal; not the act of worshiping Jesus itself, but the Christians' subsequent refusal to worship the Emperor and the other gods as the law demanded. But Christians didn't cause any material harm to society. Failing to worship Roman gods was a sin of omission, not something causing damage or danger to others. There was no grievance committed, no incident for which to apprehend them. So, for the most part, the Roman government had a "Don't Ask, Don't Tell" policy. If someone *was* brought to court on accusation of practicing Christianity, that person could prove their innocence—and avoid torture and death for the crime of atheism (refusal to worship the gods)—by cursing Christ and worshiping the Emperor. If the accused would *not* do this (and of course, Christians would not), then they were sentenced to punishment, technically for demonstrating contempt for the court's offer of clemency.[1]

There was rarely any attempt to smoke otherwise well-behaved Christians out of their neighborhoods. But this made public opinion a life-or-death situation for the Christ followers. The Christians *were* strange. Roman citizens drenched in Greco-Roman culture didn't know what to make of this group's behavior and occasionally became convinced the Christians were doing something truly heinous. You only handed your neighbor over to be killed if you really believed you must.

One common accusation was obscene sexual indiscretion. After all, this group of Christians met weekly for a meal they called "the love feast." Only the baptized were invited to this closed-door session; rumors spread that after reveling in the pleasures of food, they went on to revel in the pleasures of each other in a massive weekly orgy. Another popular accusation was that Christians ate infants. It almost made sense if you think about it. Communities heard talk of worshiping a baby boy; they heard Christians speak of eating his flesh and drinking his blood. Plus, everyone knew that Christians took abandoned babies home with them on a regular basis, so when you put two and two together . . .

Of course, *all* of this was false, misconstrued conspiracy theory. The abandoned babies were being raised in families because the Christians believed infanticide was evil, that anyone in need was to be cared for. "The love feast" was the predecessor of Communion, as well as our fellowship dinners and church potlucks—nothing at all immoral or untoward. The group of Christians who cared for each other like siblings and swore oaths against adultery were not carrying on massive orgies after sharing the Lord's Supper.

Yet for centuries, Christians were tortured and killed for these very things. Public opinion, rumor, and hearsay would rise to a pitch until folks figured they *had* to indict their Christian neighbors. After all, *what sort of people live like that?* Once in court and accused of practicing heinous acts, it wasn't enough to prove they adopted the babies and generously ate meals together. The only way out of this false accusation was to deny Christ and worship the Emperor—which they could not do.

Talk about a double bind. So, they faced imprisonment and death.

Sadly, the bizarre and deadly misunderstandings between the Christians and their Roman neighbors is just one example of a pattern playing out in human history again and again. When a group of people living among us follows different traditions and rhythms, we easily assume the worst. Suspicions turn to rumors turn to deadly accusations. Misinformation plays a huge role in transforming strangers into enemies—or rather, how we turn ourselves into *their* enemies.

RUMOR HAS IT

Since Christians were persecuted for centuries because we appeared strange to our neighbors, you would hope we would avoid perpetuating this dynamic upon others now that we've gone mainstream. But no: We harbor the same conspiracy theories about strangers in our midst that for so long were whispered about us. For centuries, Christians in Europe turned a wary eye on their Jewish neighbors, wondering about their rituals and traditions, turning differences into accusations. All too often that suspicion grew into violence, an honest belief that the *right thing to do* would be to rid the community of such likely evildoers.

Even today my country is full of rumors about certain strange groups of people, and the rumblings toward violence grow louder every day. Ironically, the types of allegation have not changed much in two thousand years. "Those people" are sexually deviant, or inclined toward violence, or eroding decent values. But just as the early Christians were building compassionate, devoted communities while being accused of orgies and cannibalism, most of the folks we hate on the basis of their deviancy are equally respectable people with slightly different traditions. It is just so easy to believe otherwise. False rumors run rampant through our information diet, like an invasive species undermining and overtaking the ecosystem. We're likely to share any report that makes our side look obviously right and "them" look stupid.

Once we've started down this road, our language takes a downturn toward dehumanization: *Only monsters would do such a thing! People like that are animals, vermin!* Daily I hear racial and ethnic minorities, immigrants, refugees, devotees of other religions, sexual minorities, or people of other political parties described as dangerous, immoral, pigs, dogs, aliens—anything but a brother or sister, a fellow human, made in the imagine of God and dearly loved. Anything but the exact person we are commanded to love and care for as we love and care for our own families.

Once our suspicions have moved to dehumanizing language, something measurable changes in our brain function. Words matter, and research bears out the dangers in our vocabulary. Men have an easier time harassing and assaulting women after using degrading words to describe them.[2] Citizens have an easier time overlooking governmental slights, abusive tactics, or even war if a campaign of dehumanizing messaging toward the targeted people group has been waged against them first.[3] As individuals and communities, we become less able to experience compassion and empathy when we place labels on entire swaths of people—and we become more comfortable perpetuating or overlooking violence toward them.

This is a carefully studied and well-documented psychological pattern in us humans, a powerful tool carefully wielded to shape public opinion and behavior. But we still fall for it, every time. We're being formed and shaped by this tendency right now. Rather than following a discipleship path of loving and caring for our neighbors and strangers, we are intentionally discipled to fear them. We inch closer and closer to the edge of violence and dehumanization by what is covered in the media, discussed online, or sometimes even taught from the pulpit. There is a grave warning for us in this, and we must be on guard. These tactics are not accidental. Society forms our character this way intentionally, and the end game is always tragedy.

The Nazis used these mind tactics before the Holocaust, as did the leaders of the Rwandan Genocide.[4] Colonists enslaved and marginalized African and indigenous peoples around the globe while carrying a cross and a Bible, claiming their actions were not sin but holy charity because the enslaved and discarded were "other" and inherently less evolved, civilized, and virtuous than the colonizers.

The tragic irony is that when we take up arms to defend ourselves against the monsters in our midst, we ourselves create the problem and become the monsters. If we follow whatever rumors sound plausible, ignorance feeds our fears; we build walls between ourselves and those we have turned into strangers. We become locked into a prison of our own making, not realizing that our own fear and hatred formed the lock, not realizing what a danger we have become to ourselves and those around us. Rumors and misinformation, followed to their conclusion, make enemies out of neighbors, out of people we could have loved, befriended, defended.

This doesn't sound like you and me, though—right? The fears we have, the suspicions we hold, the people we keep at arms' length—we're convinced we've based these decisions on truth and reasonable self-protection, even godliness. But then again, so was everyone in history who decided the right thing to do was protect themselves from their devious and dangerous neighbors (who turned out to be regular folks). The Roman citizens who turned in their Christian neighbors; the Christians who turned against their Jewish neighbors; the Rwandans who slaughtered their Tutsi neighbors. Each of these horrors—and so many more—began with the tactics we are using right now: with rumors that sounded plausible, that were bolstered until fears became tangible, until good people were *sure* they were doing the right thing.

Given this longstanding human pattern, we must find the courage to face our own fears, to confront our own biases. We must step back and ask ourselves: *Where might I be consuming untruths, or half-truths, dehumanizing and endangering people God loves? What people am I'm afraid of? What group seems dangerous, unwelcome in my neighborhood, or threatening to me or my way of life? Where do I hear or use nonhuman words used to describe humans (aliens or animals or pigs, to name just a few)?* I'm confident that if we *knew* we were doing this, we would stop; the trouble is seeing it in ourselves when it feels so justified and right.

Christians know that "love does not delight in evil but rejoices with the truth."[5] Yet we so frequently perpetuate the evil that spawns from the rumors we spread, knowingly or unknowingly. When it comes to truth there is no room for "the ends justify the means." As Christians committed to love, we must diligently seek truth—even if the truth reveals that we ourselves are the enemy.

Words matter. The comments we let slide from friends and relatives matter. The remarks we overlook in the name of keeping peace have an impact. Shame on us if we play into the hands of fearmongers. We cannot allow ourselves to speak or even think in ways that dehumanize, that allow our suspicions of difference to turn neighbors into strangers who lack the dignity of our shared humanity.

This is the pattern Jesus invited us to step away from. This is why Jesus invites us into unsafe places with joy and courage, for only a love that cannot fear death can overcome this body of death we create for ourselves. This is why Jesus places eternal judgement and eternal life in the balance of how we treat those around us, neighbor and stranger alike—for we have the tendency to form hell on earth and consign our innocent neighbors to their deaths, all because of fear.

Only as we step into the light of truth and the powerful muscle of God's love can we live together unafraid.

WE HAVE SEEN THE ENEMY

In early 2020, a young man named Ahmaud Arbery went for an afternoon jog in his own neighborhood, as he often did for exercise and enjoyment. How could this possibly be news? This happens in every neighborhood, everywhere, every day. Yet, as he ran, he was murdered by two men as they drove by, a father and son. Arbery was Black. The neighborhood he ran in was primarily white. When the two white men saw him running, they recalled that a person of color had been recently seen entering a house under construction, which sounded to them like trespassing. Somehow, this was reason enough to assume the worst about a young man with the same skin color—and they murdered him, right there on the neighborhood streets.

We have so many stories of people of color gunned down in their own communities, even their own homes. Because of the stories we tell ourselves and each other, every society learns to consider certain people strangers, someone who could not possibly belong to "us"—and innocent people pay the price of evil foolishness with their lives.

A social-media thread went viral a few years back, as a man caring for his ailing father in a British hospital live-tweeted their experience. Originally from India, the family had been British citizens for decades, the father even serving as an elected government official. Yet the man in the next hospital bed could only see them as dangerous strangers. As mother and children gathered around their sick father, speaking a mix of English and Punjabi, the man in the next bed would yell, "Gobbledegook!" or "You're in England. Speak *English.*" The son tweeted, "So my dad—flag-waving British patriot, Labour Councillor for 20 years, & former Mayor of town he lives in—is now lying in an NHS Ward with some worn-out old English bloke mumbling racist claptrap at him as they are both being fed & kept alive by hard-working immigrants. . . . [He's] loudly complaining about immigrants, while their very lives depend on being served by those same immigrants."[6] The racist comments grew more extreme, and the family asked the hospital to intervene. An administrator came and spoke to the man in the bed next door, but it made no difference. After the children left for the night their mother called, confessing she was concerned her husband—fighting for his life in the hospital—was in more danger from his neighbor than from his cancer.

Do you see the irony? With both the cancer patient and Ahmaud Arbery, it was not the man considered an intruder who was dangerous; it was the man who believed himself to be defending his country and safety who created the danger.

They perceived an enemy but failed to realize that the enemy was themselves.

GOD OF THE MARGINALIZED

I met with a pastor friend recently who was struggling with a barrage of emails from her congregants. Some pleaded with the church leadership to lead the way in fighting racism and white supremacy. Others demanded they "return to the true gospel" and not become mired in "the godless social gospel." Frustrated and discouraged, she described to me another church in her area caught in the same cross fire, that chose to take down all mention of racism in order to focus on Jesus rather than politics, lest unnecessary offense slow the cause of Christ and his Kingdom.

What a telling response this was. On one hand, we should "have nothing to do with foolish, ignorant controversies; you know that they breed quarrels."[7] But in this instance it was the influential, powerful voices whose "unnecessary offense" was avoided, while more vulnerable groups were left to suffer offense without vindication or even compassion.

Too often we avoid confronting injustices by calling them controversies and side with the powerful majority with our silence. We are concerned lest we offend those with power—but what about the harm our silence is to those without power? Avoiding conflict means allowing dehumanization of others to stand uncontested, so long as the dominant folks are comfortable. We worry more about offending powerful people with our stand than we worry about offending (or harming) less powerful brothers and sisters with our silence.

Why do we look to the powerful for our cues when Jesus

repeatedly listened to the voices in the margins at the expense of the powerful? Jesus put children at the center, rebuking his disciples for sending them away. Jesus carried on his longest-recorded conversation—a theological dialogue, no less—with a Samarian woman, to the great distress of his Jewish male disciples (and centuries of commentators since). Religious leaders were scandalized that he ate and drank with "tax collectors and sinners."[8] Jesus sided with the vulnerable, powerless, sick, suffering, sidelined, imprisoned, and demon possessed again and again, irritating the leaders of society so entirely that they sought to kill him.

If we follow Jesus into unsafe places and to unsafe people, fueled by love rather than fear, I wouldn't be surprised if we, too, end up befriending those with little influence and alienating those with religious and political power. We may not be publicly executed as Jesus was, but we may lose donors, power brokers, resources, positions, and social capital.

In her book *Fire By Night*, Melissa Florer-Bixler tells the story of Naaman from 2 Kings. Naaman is desperately ill and looking to a powerful person for help. That's how things worked in his world (and ours): Miracles can absolutely happen—if you are a person of power and wealth. But God turns the story upside down. It is a little slave girl who points Naaman to the source of healing. You couldn't get much less powerful in the ancient world than a slave girl. Working against every cultural narrative, God's prophet tells Naaman to strip down all his symbols and ceremony that prove him worthy of a miracle and stand naked and bare. It is in weakness that the miracle becomes possible.

What a shock! Naaman expected God to be represented by the powerful and wealthy. But God uses the weak things of the world to shame the strong.[9] God spoke to Naaman through a little slave girl and healed him by stripping him down.

Thousands of years later, an early critic of Christianity named Celsus leveraged the Roman cultural preference for masculine power to deride the Christians, saying:

> [The Christians] are like this: "Let no one educated, no one wise, no one sensible draw near. . . . But as for anyone ignorant, anyone stupid, anyone uneducated, anyone who is a child, let him come boldly." By the fact that they themselves admit that these people are worthy of the God, they show that they want and are able to convince only the foolish, dishonourable and stupid, and only slaves, women, and children.[10]

Celsus goes on and on, referring repeatedly to "stupid women," "little children," and various uneducated working-class folks of all kinds. To Celsus, and to many in his culture (and ours still today), it was inconceivable that the image of God be represented by a poor laundry woman. A common complaint of the Christians was that they associated with women, children, and slaves; in other words, they were emasculated, and their God was emasculated.[11] Furthermore, they were infecting society with this attitude—the idea that God would embrace and embody people as unworthy as women and slaves. Surely God would reveal *him*self as the powerful, wealthy, influential male at the top of heap, the one able to call on servants and armies and prevail against *his* enemies. Surely God is not the child of an unmarried teen mom, surely not represented by a woman or a day laborer and carpenter, surely not a friend of peasants, shepherds, and fishermen.

Or, in our own context, surely God is not living in the area code full of crowded, roach-infested apartment buildings known for poverty, gangs, and drugs but in the nicer, wealthier neighborhoods. Surely God is not found among the homeless men and women searching the streets for shelter and daily bread but with the seminary-trained men who lead big churches and bring in large donors. Surely God is not with the refugees fleeing their homeland but with the lawmakers deciding how and when to open the borders. Surely God is not a slave, a child, a woman. Our stubborn belief that God associates with social power rather than the socially vulnerable—even with thousands of years of divine revelation to the contrary—leads us to value and admire those with power and ignore, hide, or dispose of the unwanted children, people with disabilities, women, working class, elderly, and all who do not earn wealth or impose power.

Florer-Bixler writes, "The ancient rabbis have a saying: 'We do not see things as they are. We see things as we are.'"[12] Naaman assumed God works through the powerful because that is what *we* do—so we assume God does also. She continues, "I remembered that God is like that, too . . . God does not see things as they are. God sees things as God is. . . . What we learn from Naaman is that wealth and standing obscure belovedness. And when God sees us—when God sees the smallness of our lives, when God sees each of us stripped of everything, with nothing left—God sees a beloved. God is leaving everything behind and running toward us."[13]

Yes, God sees us—all of us, all of creation—as beloved. Not because we are wonderful but because God is love. This depth of God's character is our foundation and our saving grace, for it is God's kindness that brings us to repentance; it is God's love that reaches out to us and changes us.

How do we learn to see this world that God calls beloved? If we see as we are . . . then what are we? These days, we often see a scary world because we are afraid. We look at our neighborhoods and country and see not what is there but what we are. We are afraid, and so we see reasons to fear. We are envious, so we see strangers coming to take what we have worked for, longed for. We solve our worries by turning to wealthy and powerful protectors and lose the ability to see the weak, marginalized, vulnerable, the essential workers, the children, the disabled, the elderly. We hide away those we don't want to think about or threaten and remove those we fear. We create strangers out of brothers and sisters. We see danger and hatred coming toward us because we have allowed our fears to ferment, because we are drenched in hate. We see threatening strangers encroaching on our own rights and ways of life because we have lost the ability to see in our fellow humans the dignity of brothers and sisters made in the image of God.

Why are we afraid? How can we love and open ourselves up to be loved?

How can we learn to see what the God of love sees?

BRAVE STEPS

EXPANDING JESUS' DESCRIPTION OF "NEIGHBOR" to encompass anyone we encounter who has a need will not come easily. Not only will our beliefs need to change but also our language, our priorities, the way we spend our time and energy, the posture we take toward the world around us. Whether you are reading alone or with a group, these questions, practices, and activities are designed to help you explore what it looks like for Christians to actively love, not fear, strangers in our real lives and communities.

REFLECT AND DISCUSS

How does Jesus answer the question "Who is my neighbor?" in the story of the Good Samaritan? In what ways was his answer culturally and religiously off-putting? How do you think he would answer if we were asking?

What sorts of people are you afraid of? What, specifically, are your concerns?

What messages about "strangers" do you hear in the media, at church, or in your community? What about foreigners, like immigrants and refugees? How do these messages fit or clash with what the Bible says about our responsibility to strangers and newcomers?

There are real risks in helping strangers in need; there are also real risks in normalizing *not* helping strangers. What are some of these risks? How can we balance this and make wise, Christ-honoring decisions?

What dehumanizing language do you hear (or use) for certain groups of people? What rumors and suspicions do you associate with these groups? How can you practice seeing these people as dearly loved children of God?

If Jesus were a baby today, what family, country, and circumstance would he choose to be born into, do you think?

In what ways have you viewed strangers with fear? How can you begin to view them with love?

PRACTICE

- Pull out a journal or drawing paper, and spend time reflecting on this question: What does God see when he looks at the world? Jot down the things that come to mind, or draw them.

    Then get more specific. What does God see when he looks at *me* (or *us*, if you are doing this with a group)? What does God see when he looks at powerful, wealthy people? What does God see when he looks at under-resourced or oppressed people? What about senators and celebrities? What about migrants crossing the border or people with disabilities? Imagine someone who seems strange or dangerous to you, then ask: What does God see when he looks at _____?

Now, look at your paper. How does what you've written or drawn differ from how *you* see these people or groups of people?

- Make a list of all the strangers whose work and service made your day possible. For example: janitors, cooks, delivery people, bus drivers, cashiers. Or, gather friends and family for a meal and consider all the strangers who made this meal possible: farmers, field workers, truckers, factory workers, warehouse workers . . . and more! Children in the group can draw pictures. Express gratitude for the strangers who have made this day or meal possible. The next time you see someone working in these capacities, say "Thank you."

- Visit a Christian congregation that is different from your own in language, race, ethnicity, or denomination. Introduce yourself as a guest, share Communion if appropriate, or visit the fellowship hall. If people reach out to you, rejoice in the family of God that transcends so many human differences. If people do not reach out to you, consider what it feels like to be a stranger and reflect on how you can offer hospitality in your own spaces.

- Inform yourself about the laws, policies, and realities of immigration in your area. World Relief is one organization that provides reputable information with Christian service in mind.

- Check with your city, school district, or library to find out how you and your church can connect to and support newcomers in your community. Find out who is doing this work effectively and learn from them. Is there a faith-based community-service organization serving a population of people in your community that you identified as a "stranger" in these exercises? Reach out to that organization and engage with a learning posture.

LOOK AND LISTEN

- *The Good Samaritan* painting by Ferdinand Hodler[1]
- *The Hospitality of Abraham* painting by Andrei Rublev
- "Citizens" song by Jon Guerra

Find this art or music online, then spend some time sitting with it. What do you see and hear? What invitation is God offering you through this?

INTERMISSION

LET ME STOP FOR A MOMENT and check on you, dear reader. We have had a steep climb so far, and we have a steeper road yet ahead. Will you pause for a moment, take a breath, and check in with yourself? Take a moment to pray. Find me on the internet and send me a message if that helps.[1] We cannot do this alone.

Remember friend, you are surrounded by love, by God's presence and kindness, by the great cloud of witnesses who have gone before us and now cheer us on. You are surrounded by compassion. You are not alone. None of us can complete this mission by ourselves, so God calls us together. That is why the pronouns in the Bible are plural: We are part of a body, each doing our own small part. We are hands. Feet. Brains. Hearts. Working together to make this small change that changes

---

[1] You can find my website and social-media handles on page 201. I would love to hear from you.

everything. Remember what the *Didache* instructed the early Christians? Do as much as you can. Don't allow fear to tell you the choices are *be perfect* or *never begin. Do as much as you can.*

Remember first and foremost the words of 1 John 4:18: "There is no fear in love." There is no need to panic. God is not abusive, not waiting for us to fail so he can unleash his anger and rid himself of us. God is love. God's compassion and loving-kindness never end. God has given us work to do out of loving relationship and out of his joyful, creative plan of redemption. God invites us into a new family of people who receive this gift of love and invite others to join—with our words of good news, and also with our active love.

Where we are going next is harder still: God's command to love our enemies. Surely this is the hardest task we will ever take on. But we are on this side of the Resurrection, and we are part of a team. Jesus and the Spirit remain with us always. We have no reason to fear, for death—and all the weapons of the powerful and oppressive that rely on fear—have no power over us now.

Take heart, friend. You are loved with an everlasting love.

Here we go.

ENEMIES

An enemy is a person whose story we have not yet heard.

ANONYMOUS

THESE WERE STRANGE TIMES. The new church in Jerusalem was growing, spreading. But there was opposition. They had enemies. Boy, did they have enemies.

There was a disciple named Stephen, known for his wisdom and miracles. He spoke with the voice of God; he performed signs and wonders. It was said that Stephen was full of God's grace and power, that where he went, the church grew.

This was not what their enemies liked to see. How does one stand against someone like this? It is the tale as old as time: Stephen was falsely accused and brutally killed.

The young man overseeing his death was named Saul, and Saul was only getting started. After Stephen, he unleashed persecution over the entire church, going from house to house, dragging men and women to prison. Saul was relentless; his intent was to destroy the church—and he nearly did.

But he did something else as well: Saul scattered the people all over the countryside as they fled for their lives. As they dispersed, the Christians preached the word of God wherever they went. One of those places was Samaria, home of the people Jews considered traitors, heretics, religious and political enemies.

But though the Samaritans were despised, they were not hunting Christian heads. So as the Christians fled for their lives, some of them passed through Samaria, receiving their hospitality. As they preached the good news of Jesus, many in Samaria believed. Can you imagine? Men and women whose vendetta went back generations were now adopted brothers and sisters; ancient enemies, reconciled. The Jewish Christians baptized the new Samaritan Christians, sending word to Jerusalem for the apostles to come lay their hands on these former enemies and convey to them the Holy Spirit.

More and more and more Samaritans joined with their enemies to form a new family in Christ. Dividing walls were coming down in Jesus' name. In Christ, the old ways of *us* and *them* were fading away.

Meanwhile, Saul, their primary enemy, was in pursuit, "breathing out murderous threats against the Lord's disciples."[1] Destroying the church in Jerusalem was not enough; his aim was to track down the Christians, every last man, woman, and child. Saul spent his time on the road, going wherever the Christians might be.

But what he found was not exactly what he was looking for. Suddenly overcome by a bright light, Saul fell to the ground right there on the road, blind. The light had plunged him into darkness. Then a voice sounded, demanding an answer: "Saul! Why do you persecute me?" Saul had no answer. Now disabled, he and his men hunkered down in a nearby town; for three days he could not see anything, or eat anything, or drink anything.

On the third day, God appeared to a local Christian named Ananias, telling him to visit Saul. Ananias protested, as you might expect. This was the man they were running *from*, not *toward*. "I have heard of this man, who hunts and harms your people," pointed out Ananias. "He is here to persecute and arrest us!"

Still, Ananias went. He cared for and prayed for this enemy, as God asked. He laid his hands on Saul, healing his eyes and his body—and his soul. Saul was filled with the Holy Spirit and was baptized.

Back to Jerusalem went Saul, straight to the disciples and apostles. Only this time, not to kill them but to join them.

To say the church could not believe their eyes is an understatement.

These were strange times. It was disorienting, all these enemy lines crossing and blurring. It was hard to know who to be afraid of anymore.

CHAPTER 10

A HARD TEACHING

WHEN DANIEL'S UNCLE WAS KILLED, everyone agreed: The family duty of revenge fell to Daniel. The deceased man's son was only six years old; his brother (Daniel's father) was already too old and weak. There was no question *if* vengeance was required, merely to whom the task should fall.

So Daniel gathered a few allies and went to fight for his family's honor.

Daniel's family couldn't remember where this generations-long conflict started, though the story goes it began when someone's pig ruined another person's garden. One man confronted the other, and things got ugly. Both men took to arms, and one killed the other. The bereaved family took revenge—and the rest is history. Though Daniel doesn't know how many people have died on either side, he can count seventeen dead in the name of revenge from the past few years.[1]

For much of human history, this is how justice was met: an eye for an eye, carried out privately between families. Trouble is, where does it end? When the balance of justice requires payment for sin, there can be no end to violence and bloodshed.

Today, most of us are not honor-bound to sustain a cycle of generational vengeance, but these patterns are embedded in our sense of right and wrong all the same. We understand which ideological, religious, or political tribe we belong to, and which group of people we despise, resist, or at least look down on with contempt. Many of us have been deeply wounded by direct acts of violence or systems of ongoing aggression and oppression. We can clearly articulate the person or people we have learned to take sides against, or who have taken sides against us.

From partisanship to gang violence to deadly international warfare, our commitment to the cycles of vengeance are all but unbreakable, spanning generations. What power could possibly turn the tide?

Learning to love our enemies would be the challenge of a lifetime.

YOU HAVE HEARD IT SAID

Jesus sat down on the mountainside, surrounded by students and disciples. He taught them the Law and Prophets, carefully placing his own teaching inside their sacred tradition. "You have heard it said . . ." Jesus said, quoting the law. "But I say to you . . ." he continued, filling in his commentary, explaining that the spirit of the law must be fulfilled alongside the letter of the law. God's intent was not merely avoidance of murder, falsehood, and adultery; the law was given to form a faithful people who do not use and abuse each other, who do not let anger, greed, and lusts grow out of hand.

Then: "You have heard that it was said, 'Love your neighbor.'"

Yes, they had heard, just as we have. We have seen in these pages how God commands us to love and care for our communities as we care for our own families. Even strangers fall within Jesus' definition of "neighbor" now. We know this. *Doing* it is the challenge.

Then Jesus continued: "But I tell you, love your enemies and pray for those who persecute you."[2]

Oh Jesus, Son of the living God, have mercy on us.[3] This is a hard teaching. Are there *no* boundaries to your love?

The throwback passage Jesus refers to here is Leviticus 19, where the Law goes into detail on how one ought to treat a neighbor: Don't cheat or rob them, don't hold back money you owe, don't obscure the truth when judging between them, don't endanger your neighbor's life or spread lies about them. Don't hate or hold grudges, "but love your neighbor as yourself. I am the LORD,"[4] God says. Yes, this is all good sense. Hard as it may be to live out, we all agree in theory.

That was not what Jesus taught this day. This day, Jesus had a "but": *But I tell you, love your enemies and pray for those who persecute you.*

When my seminary professor came to this passage in his lecture, he paused. He had previously shared with us some of the atrocities he witnessed in his life, the violence he had lived through, the pain he had seen. "This one is really hard," he said softly. "I think this is the hardest of Jesus' teaching."

Jesus knew the weight of his words. He and his friends

suffered under real enemies. They were poor, oppressed by unjust economics, and occupied by a violent foreign empire. Jesus wasn't just talking. He knew what his words meant.

This, according to Jesus, is the "why": Those who love their enemies and pray for their persecutors are true children of God, the Father.[5]

In other words, the essence of Jesus' teaching is about God, and God's character. This is what God was creating and building on earth in the first place, how we bear the image of God in the world, how we reflect the Creator to each other—a weighty responsibility we must take seriously. We must not show the world a violent, vengeful God. God is the sort of God, Jesus insisted, who sends love and provision, sunshine and rain, not only to those who love him, who seek and serve him, but to *everyone*. All of us, *all of us*, are dearly loved children of God. As ambassadors for God, it matters how we represent God.

Jesus embedded this hardest of commands within the most bewilderingly delightful truth—God works for the good of his creation, even those who have set themselves against him. God is love, and in love there is no fear, no darkness at all. Our God is not a capricious, vindictive deity who keeps score and bides his time for revenge. We are set free to love as God loves because we are already, fully, completely loved by God ourselves. All of us.

After all, as Jesus pointed out, if we love only those who love us in return, we really just love ourselves, don't we? Like a Christmas party where everyone exchanges twenty-dollar gift cards, we may as well just get a gift for ourselves. God says, "We are not having that kind of party. Go out, cross boundaries and enemy lines, and work for the good of those who will not give you the time of day. Make things better for the people you cannot stand. Give to those who would rather steal from you than sit with you."

God isn't out of touch with our pain and troubles—quite the opposite. God has seen generation after generation spiral through cycles of revenge and violence, returning hate for hate and evil for evil, our human tendency to take his good gifts of relationship and turn them into hell on earth. Someone must stop the cycle. Someone has to put their foot down and say, "No. Another generation of hatred will not solve this problem."

In Jesus, God is that person. God stops the cycle, taking the pain on Godself.

Or, as Jesus put it in the Gospel of Luke:

To you who are listening I say: Love your enemies, do good to those who hate you, bless those who curse you, pray for those who mistreat you. If someone slaps you on one cheek, turn to them the other also. If someone takes your coat, do not withhold your shirt from them. Give to everyone who asks you, and if anyone takes what belongs to you, do not demand it back. Do to others as you would have them do to you.

If you love those who love you, what credit is that to you? Even sinners love those who love them. And if you do good to those who are good to you, what credit is that to you? Even sinners do that. And if you lend to those from whom you expect repayment, what credit is that to you? Even sinners lend to sinners, expecting to be repaid in full. But love your enemies, do good to them, and lend to them without expecting to get anything back. Then your reward will be great, and you will be children of the Most High, because he is kind to the ungrateful and wicked. Be merciful, just as your Father is merciful.[6]

What strikes me most is how very wide God's net is, how clear the call is on our lives if we choose to follow him, to represent him. There is no line beyond which his love and mercy will not go. For us, the heirs of this mercy, he outlines an incredibly unintuitive way to live. When someone curses you? Bless them. When someone harms you? Do something good for them. Hits you and you feel like punching back? Let them hit you a second time. When someone steals something from you? Don't even ask for it back. Offer them even more than they took.

Not because we are worthless doormats, but because we are already filled to overflowing with an everlasting love.

WHO IS MY ENEMY?

At first glance, the command *Love your enemies and pray for those who persecute you* sounds like a poetic way of saying the same thing twice. But in fact, these are two different sets of people. "Those who persecute you"—well, that's pretty clear. These people actively seek our harm. But the word Jesus uses for *enemies* is not a noun (a certain group of people), but an adjective (the way we describe people). It could be translated "hated people" or "odious people."[7] In other words, enemies are the people *I* hate. Those who are odious *to me*. In addition to praying for those trying to harm us, we are to actively love those who repulse us.[8]

This strikes me as two very different sets of muscles, and Jesus prescribes two different exercises. The people we hate, we are to *agapaō*, the verb form of *agapē*. This is not a warm fuzzy feeling but action; this love is a verb. Agapē includes a demonstration of goodwill, "regard the welfare of," "to welcome, to entertain, to be fond of, to love dearly."[9] When I encounter someone (or a group of someones) who make my nose wrinkle and my head shake, my next step should be to actively serve them.

Who is your enemy, the people who are "odious" or "distasteful" to you? If your community is anything like mine, members of a political party or religion are on this list, people from a certain race or ethnicity, a region of the country, or an economic class. Someone whose lifestyle or values you disagree with. Jesus assumes that this experience of dislike is common to all of us. Then he prescribes love as the antidote, a daily regimen replacing disdain with dignity and hospitality. This is an exercise we will need to practice intentionally and indefinitely, every day of our lives, lest contempt destroy our love.

The second group Jesus mentions, those who persecute us, is the hardest of all. These people are not merely distasteful but dangerous, seeking to harm us openly or covertly, legally or illegally. Jesus does not ask us to agapē (actively love) these people but to pray for them. Some enemies must be loved from a distance. A woman fleeing her violent ex-husband should not meet him for coffee. A man testifying against his assailant should not either. But we can pray. We can refuse to perpetuate the cycles of vengeance, hatred, and fear.

Elsewhere, Jesus taught us to turn the other cheek and give our sweater to the thief who stole our coat. But Jesus didn't bring casseroles to the people in Jerusalem plotting his death. He spent his time serving those the world overlooked and despised, and when the killers caught up to him, Jesus prayed for them—for their eyes to see what they were doing, and for God to forgive them—even as he died at their hands.

We must wash the feet of those we cannot stand, but our first—and possibly only—step to loving a violent person is an ongoing posture of prayer. And frankly, this is hard enough.

I'm curious who came to mind as the disciples listened to Jesus' teaching. Who were their enemies? These families lived in an occupied nation, and their rulers used terrorism and violence to remind them of their place. Rome perfected the ancient brutality of crucifixion and used it for mass executions in the lands they occupied—particularly the areas around Judea. Around the time Jesus was born, a Roman general crucified two thousand men in a mass execution near Galilee[10]—and this was just one of many graphic, horrific examples Jesus and his followers lived through, personally, within their own local community. Jesus' command to love not only their neighbors but to pray for those persecuting them went all the way down deep, touching the scars of trauma, generational wounds of suffering.

Pray for them, Jesus said. Pray and do not curse.

At the same time, there were folks Jesus' followers disdained and looked down upon. Hurting people hurt people; that's how it works. It doesn't take the strength of an empire's army to make life difficult for the people you detest. For this, Jesus prescribes more than prayer: His followers must *agapaō*, actively serve, welcome, and care for those they hate. This goes far beyond ceasing harm, far beyond even toleration. Jesus commands us to put time and energy behind our love, seeking the good of the people we dislike and working for the benefit of those we consider enemies.

It was hard enough when Jesus told us to care for our neighbors as we care for our own families. Then he clarified that by "neighbor" he meant anyone—even strangers—who had a need. Now, he asks us to turn our enemies into neighbors too.[11]

RUBBER, MEET THE ROAD

I was sitting on the floor of our church sanctuary, watching my baby brother chew cardboard books, when the doors flew open and two men burst in. Standing just feet from me, they silenced the sounds of worship and hollered an urgent proclamation: The United States had fallen to Communists. We had been overtaken. It was time to choose if we would die for Christ or deny him and save our lives.

This moment is forever etched into my mind, but the details are fuzzy. I was very young. I can only assume the adults and older children in the room understood this was a skit, but all I knew was that men I loved and trusted were shouting that my life was over, that all safety was gone, that the worst had happened. Our enemies had come, just as we feared.

My childhood church had one thing right: We did have enemies out in the world. Our country did, as all countries do. Christians do, as all communities do. But perhaps the drill we needed was not preparing how to fight or flight, deny Christ or die. We needed to be drilled in loving our enemies, praying for the people about to persecute us, following Jesus down this hard road by actively serving those we despise. In my childhood faith I was warned of all the outsiders who wanted to harm us, take away our rights, or kill us. I was never taught what it might look like to love and serve these hypothetical people. I would have benefited from learning self-defense and common-sense protection in childhood, but fearmongering did not provide me with those tools either. All I was given was a world view in which we ought always imagine and fear danger, even when none is nearby.

Yet these enemies never materialized. What materialized instead was a generation of Christians turned, by tens of thousands, into people ruled by fear. I can't help but wonder how the American church would be different today if we had spent as much time and energy praying for our enemies and serving those we despise as we did (and do) reminding each other to be afraid.

In his book *The Cross and the Lynching Tree*, James Cone considers the centuries that white Americans worshiped the crucified Jesus but couldn't see they were practicing the same reign of terror that killed Jesus—exerting power over the powerless by hanging innocent people on a tree. How great is our ability to self-deceive! Though I did not live in that time or that place, I am just as human as these men and women were, just as likely to play the evil villain while believing I am righteously on God's side. In what ways have I been formed to see violence against my enemy as a valid stand for righteousness, when in fact my community is wielding unjust power against the powerless?

Whether our enemies are far away or close at hand, the day to start praying for them is today. Prayer does not surrender the fight against injustice. We are commanded to spend our energy serving those who are despised *and* praying for those who incite violence.

Jesus didn't just give lip service to this teaching. He spent a lifetime serving those who were despised. And when he, too, was nailed to a cross as a public warning against resisting evil, he prayed for his enemies just as he had prayed for his friends. His disciples struggled with this, as we do. We have seen how afraid they were, and for good reason. But after the Resurrection something changed. After the Resurrection, after the Spirit of God came over them, love conquered even their hatred and fear of enemies.

LOVING-KINDNESS

The thing with discipleship is it doesn't happen overnight—or by accident. We are formed into followers of Jesus by the power of the Spirit and practice, practice, practice. Loving our enemies is an enormous ask, and it takes time to build those muscles. We need tangible, practical things to move our hearts and minds in the right direction, step-by-step.

An ancient practice called Loving-Kindness Meditation may be a helpful starting place. This is a long-term practice, not something you can do all in one day; aligning our revenge-inclined hearts to God will take a lifetime of surrendering. But the first step is to start.

During a time of quiet prayer, remember the loving, nurturing heart of God—the same loving-kindness the Bible teaches and Jesus embodies. Imagine a space filled with this love, then picture yourself in it. This first step may come easily to you, or it may take a good bit of time—days or weeks of practicing if you view God as abusive or vindictive.

Once you have grown comfortable in this spacious place of love, bring to mind others that you love. Begin widening the space to include them. Then, recall people you don't know well, or have neutral feelings about, and allow the space of God's grace and love to cover them too. Finally, bring to mind enemies, one at a time. Don't begin this process with the person who has harmed you the most; choose instead someone who frustrates or annoys you. Then, bit by bit, day by day, expand this circle a bit further in your mind. If the process becomes too traumatic, go back to the beginning and rest in God's spacious love. Contact a pastor, spiritual director, or therapist if you need professional help. Take your time. It may take weeks to progress to this stage of the exercise, and it may take years to complete this step. If we have trouble learning to receive God's love ourselves, how much harder will it be to expand this love to our enemies, even within our imagination?

Over the months and years, practice this meditation until you can see God's love and kindness surrounding you and your loved ones, even strangers, and then yes, even enemies.

Of course, God's love already covers us all, already, right now. But practicing these prayers with words and pictures, day after day, allows God to renew our minds—including our neurological pathways and thought patterns—and change our hearts. This, in turn, will change our behavior, which Jesus seems to think could change the world.[12]

So to recap, here are the people whom I am called by God's mercy to love, and, in some cases, actively help and care for:

- my family
- my community
- strangers and foreigners
- anyone who needs help
- anyone who doesn't belong here
- anyone I cannot stand to be around
- anyone I *strongly* disagree with, including those I believe are damaging my country or faith; and
- anyone trying to harm me.

And here is the list of people that, as a Christian, I am free to ignore and hate:

-

-

-

(The list is empty, friends. Not one person on earth meets this criteria).

CHAPTER 11

OUR NONVIOLENT GOD

THE SONGS I SANG in childhood Sunday school class were rather, um, violent. I grew up singing these tunes every week, so I didn't realize how horrifying they sounded until I was older, entertaining my college friends during late-night study sessions. They were simply the soundtrack of my childhood. My favorite—and the most shocking to my friends—told the story of Ananias and Saphira. In a cheerful, upbeat melody with hand motions and dance steps, this children's song ends by gleefully announcing that the two cheaters "both dropped dead."[1]

Another favorite song recounted David's battle with Goliath. It included a sing-song chorus about carefully choosing the deadliest weapons, as well as a cheerful description of the attack. Of course, it also playfully incorporated hand motions and ended with a giddy pronouncement of death.

I have several more gruesome songs up my sleeve, but I think you get the idea. These Sunday school jingles nearly all end with someone dropping dead.

As wildly and utterly inappropriate as these songs were for my preschool classroom, I have a theological issue to throw in with the developmental concerns. We highlight violent stories in the Bible and glorify them without exploring the cultural context or the theological meaning they were written to convey. It's all too easy to pick and choose stories and verses from the Bible and conclude that the Lord is a warrior who will fight *our* enemies, to the death, and furthermore, send our enemies to eternal death. You and I, on the other hand, will be vindicated and rewarded handsomely both in this life and in the life to come. In other words, cherry-picked Bible stories become fodder for our assumption that God has the same enemies we do and isn't afraid to use lethal force against them to benefit us, his truly beloved ones. It's a very convenient deity to believe in.

But if we remove our self-focus from these stories and look at the character of *God* revealed in the Bible—and the arc of redemption unveiled in the Bible—something far different emerges.

NOAH AND THE NONVIOLENT GOD

Noah's story is a prime example of biblical violence sanitized and popularized into a narrative for children. I bucked the trend in nursery decor when my kids were small and flatly refused to hang any arks or two-by-two parades of elephants and lions in my babies' room. Somehow, the mass destruction of 99 percent of human and nonhuman life on earth didn't strike me as a good bedtime story, even if it does feature a menagerie of animals and a rainbow of color. (And yes, I know several upbeat songs about the ark, with millions dropping dead by the end.)

We tell the flood story as though the moral is God entirely fed up with wickedness, not hesitating to use violence against creation. But according to the Bible, the end of Noah's story leads us to this conclusion: God, our God, *the* God, rejects violence, will *not* attack his enemies, not even those who have set themselves against him. Looking past our cheerful preschool songs of carnage and genocide, we find that this ancient text teaches an eternal theological truth.

At the end of the genealogy that begins the story, we find Lamach naming his newborn son Noah and saying, "Out of the ground that the LORD has cursed, this one shall bring us relief from our work and from the painful toil of our hands."[2] The name "Noah" means "to comfort" or "rest," so in this overlooked baby naming we find the key to the entire story (and the gospel): Out of the sin-cursed ground will come relief, and out of the destruction and consequences of our broken choices will come life.

In preparation for the coming deluge, Noah is instructed to build his ark, then gather the animals and his family. The rains come, then go, and eventually they are set free, beginning life anew on the earth. To the ancient imagination, "blotting out" with water meant a return to chaos. In the original creation story, God shaped beautiful, useful function from watery chaos; here the process was reversed. Life on earth was not so much drowned but retaken by the forces of chaos to be re-created into something beautiful and useful once again.

It quickly becomes apparent, however, that this new creation is just as bent on being enemies with God as the original. So, what has all this been about? How is Lamech's prediction to be fulfilled, and how does Noah's life bring relief, comfort, or rest—much less redemption?

The answer lies in the real main character of the story—Yahweh. While we focus on Noah, his ark, and his animals, the real action happens within God himself. The question this story answers is: How will God deal with human violence? At the outset of the story, the Bible tells us that God is sending this flood to blot out life from the earth *because of humankind's incurable wickedness.*[3] At the end, God sets aside his weapon—a bow—in the sky, vowing never again to strike down all living things. The reason God gives for this promise? *The intentions of the human heart is evil from their youth.*[4]

It's a shocking twist. God's strategy toward humankind takes an entire 180-degree turn. People remain the same, but God's response to our unrelenting violence changes forever: from "therefore, I will destroy them" to "therefore, I will never destroy them."

In this story we see the heart of God not as a warrior destroying enemies but as a grieved parent seeking restored relationship. The story speaks poignantly of God's sorrow; unlike the gods of the ancient world, God is not dispassionate to our suffering. But the consequences of this pain God ultimately resolves to put upon himself.

This is worth sitting in for a minute. We know this about God, right? But do we *know* it?

If God's plan was to destroy sin and evil through violence,

he utterly failed. There is no human repentance or evidence of change in this story; rather, quite the opposite. What changes is God and his approach to humanity. The early chapters of Genesis set up a constant tension: God makes someone beautiful and good, humans set themselves against God, the wonderful plan falls apart. So God makes a new plan. And then repeat. We see it in the garden, then with Cain and Abel, then with Noah, and at the tower of Babel. In these stories that form the basis of Hebrew, Jewish, and Christian understanding of reality, God keeps making a new path toward life, even though we blatantly and consistently declare ourselves his enemies. The Flood story is the climax and results in God's decisive resolution: Creation will not behave as a friend of God, so what will God do?

God changes his strategy. He will not give up his intentions for goodness even as he grieves our choices. Placing his bow in the sky, God commits to be faithful and nonviolent *even though* we still prove utterly unfaithful and violent. Humankind has proven hopeless; hence hope must come from God.

God calls forth Abram and Sarai and starts the ball rolling on a long-term plan of peace.

Do God's plans fail? Did God actually change his mind about humanity and the entire earth, some six thousand years ago? No, the Bible tells us that our Creator is the Alpha and Omega, the beginning and the end, unchanging and sovereign over all things. But the story is here to convey a truth we struggle to grasp. We just can't shake the image of God as a violent force bent on annihilating humanity. Flood stories were common in the ancient world, long before Genesis was written down, long even before the patriarchs and matriarchs began to form the Hebrew nation. But by the inspiration of God's Spirit, the Hebrews told the old story *this* way, driving home the truth of God's character: *God is not a violent God.* All the way back in the beginning, God loudly declared himself to be the God of nonviolence. Knowing full well that we have made ourselves his enemies, God made an irrevocable covenant with all living things and all generations.

Hell-bent on violence as God knows we are, we continue telling God's story as though it were bad news: God will destroy his enemies (who are our enemies) and even this precious world he created. It's just a matter of time! It's all gonna burn!

But the message passed down to us in the Scripture is this: God will love and nurture even when we have hated and killed. He will rebuild and redeem even where we have destroyed.[5]

THE SUFFERING SERVANT

With all the NC-17 level violence that continues throughout the Bible, we might be forgiven for missing the forest of God's nonviolence through the trees of war, genocide, slavery, misogyny, and sexual violence. But it is there nonetheless, even if our modern eyes are not trained to fluently understand the culture, religion, and writings of the ancient world.

The early Hebrews worshiped Yahweh alone, considering their fidelity to him of utmost importance. But this loyalty took place in a world populated by countless other gods—or so they assumed—Baal and Asherah, to name a few. The Hebrews saw their relationship to Yahweh as I see my marriage vows: I am bonded to my husband exclusively, but my loyalty to him does not rest on a mistaken belief that there are no other men on earth. Yahweh was Israel's one-and-only God, but other nations had their gods as well. The temptation—and warning—was to not chase after any god besides God.

But then, in the book of Isaiah, we find the first expression of what will become the prevailing view of Judaism: monotheism. *There is only one God.* Not merely "one God for us" or "only one God worth mentioning" but *one*, period. Before Isaiah, Yahweh was understood as clearly superior; after Isaiah, Yahweh is understood as the one and only God existing.

This God—whom we now know is *the* God—had always revealed himself as compassionate, abounding in steadfast love and mercy. Yahweh used these words to describe himself back at Mount Sinai when he introduced himself to Moses and entered an official relationship with the Hebrews. These words God chose—*gracious and compassionate, slow to anger*, and *abounding in steadfast love and mercy*—echo throughout the Law, the Prophets, the history narratives, and the Psalms over and over, again and again.[6] Add Yahweh's long-understood character to the newly understood belief in monotheism and it equals something truly earth-shattering: This compassionate and merciful God is *the* God, over all that is and shall be. Compassion and mercy is the foundation of reality, the beginning and the end.

Isaiah is also where we find "The Servant Songs," four poems that describe a suffering servant who lifts his face to God for relief but does not strike back in self-defense or retaliation. Isaiah referred to exiled Israel in these verses, but Christians have always read them as fulfilled in Jesus, God-made-flesh: "He was oppressed, and he was afflicted, yet he opened not his mouth;

like a lamb that is led to the slaughter, and like a sheep that before its shearers is silent, so he opened not his mouth."[7]

And indeed, this is just who we meet in Jesus. When God takes on flesh and moves into the neighborhood,[8] when we meet the embodiment of God's character, it is exactly like this. Jesus, the Son of God, loves and confronts and heals and challenges his enemies, ultimately pouring himself out, offering his life that they might have life. In case we missed it in Creation, in the Flood story, in the Law, and in the Prophets, Jesus shows us God's true character *in the flesh*. God, the one God, the Alpha and Omega, is the Suffering Servant, who will provide for his enemies and will not strike back in retaliation.

If we were on the fence about the nonviolent, merciful character of God, or Jesus' teaching on love over violence and fear, the Sermon on the Mount erases any lingering doubt. Jesus addresses the people of God—those who followed the Torah as well as those of us who will be grafted in at his Resurrection— with a vision for living into God's Kingdom:

> "You have heard that it was said, 'Eye for eye, and tooth for tooth.' But I tell you, do not resist an evil person. If anyone slaps you on the right cheek, turn to them the other cheek also. And if anyone wants to sue you and take your shirt, hand over your coat as well. If anyone forces you to go one mile, go with them two miles. Give to the one who asks you, and do not turn away from the one who wants to borrow from you."[9]

> "Be merciful, just as your Father is merciful."[10]

Having removed the resources of violence from their tool-box, Jesus sends his disciples out without a staff, money, or even shoes. God's Kingdom will not be represented by patriots or zealots. God's people will embody an entirely different way of being.[11] The vision of Isaiah is being fulfilled in Jesus, the image of the one true God, the Suffering Servant. In his Kingdom swords are recycled into farming equipment so that all may be nurtured without fear, our tables filled with abundance rather than talk of war.

This is the way of the Lord, as the prophets declared and Jesus demonstrated.[12] It isn't that our evil, violent ways aren't weighty and destructive—they are. It isn't that God can simply gloss over our sin—he can't and won't. The point is that violence does not solve the problems of violence. God has chosen to suffer rather than condemn, to redeem through sacrifice rather than destruction.

Yet still we imagine God an angry, vengeful destroyer who will torture his enemies (and ours) and smile while doing it. So I return again to my question: What fears motivate us to seek a fearful God of vengeance, rather than a loving God of mercy? Are we afraid to follow the God who died for his enemies?

CROSSING THE LINE

Don't let all this talk of love and mercy lead you to confuse Jesus, God-made-man, with a pushover nice guy, floating through life in a semi-meditative stance. Jesus had passion. Jesus had enemies. He made no attempt to fly under the radar. Jesus' love confronted sin, evil, and injustice with his words, behavior, life, and death. He did not neatly follow rules or play it safe: Jesus crossed all the lines. There's a difference between violence and disruption, and Jesus disrupted hierarchies and oppressors with courageous, compassionate confrontation.

Jesus was not a "good" person on the sidelines, but neither was he a violent zealot. Jesus' message did not fit anywhere on the spectrum of silence-to-violence but demonstrated a third way: disruptive nonviolent resistance rooted and powered in love. Jesus went to the margins of society, to unsafe people and places. Jesus visited the hometowns of his persecutors (those with power to harm and silence him) and his enemies (those his community had been taught to despise). He healed and helped those in need, argued with and confronted those abusing power, and prayed for those who plotted his death. He broke bread with and washed the feet of the man who would soon betray him.

Too often we describe "good Christians" as those who stay inside the lines. We love to draw solid boundaries between us and "those sinful people" we're nothing like. But Christians cannot live separate lives, safely removed from the people we're called to love. Jesus did not fly under the radar, and neither can we.

In his "Letter from Birmingham Jail" Martin Luther King wrote that "We will have to repent in this generation not merely for the hateful words and actions of the bad people but for the appalling silence of the good people."[13] This indictment has not lost its resounding truth over the years. We feel good about ourselves when we denounce sins and point fingers. But Jesus did not gossip on the sidelines. Jesus *engaged.* As Paul writes to the church in Romans, our "love [*agapē*] must be sincere. Hate what is evil; cling to what is good." Those are strong, active words. Our love cannot be lip service. How do we accomplish this? By blessing, not cursing, those who persecute us. We do not repay anyone evil for evil. We do not take revenge, but if our enemy is hungry, we feed him; and if he is thirsty, we give him something to drink. We are not overcome by evil, but we overcome evil with good.[14]

Notice how engaged and busy these words are. We are not invited merely to separate from evil, or frown at evil, or dissociate with evil, but *overcome* evil. Not through violence, power, or revenge but through *active goodness* and *blessing*. Not only do we pray for our enemies, we bless them, feed them, offer them a drink. We don't wash our hands of evil; we get our hands dirty.

This teaching—together with so many others in the Gospels and Epistles—forms the foundation of the Christian way in the world: following our merciful, nonviolent God and our suffering Savior, we actively resist evil with love. We do not love quietly in the corner, from a place of safety and purity; we love loudly, disruptively. As a community our love should instigate all sorts of social and political upheaval as we actively and forcefully *resist* the evils in our society (including in our churches), overcoming them with love and goodness.

And we do so without fear, for what can humans do to us? As we have seen, the powerful wield death as a weapon so that fear will stop us from rocking the boat. *But Jesus' resurrection changed all that.* We are living in the post-Resurrection world. Death—and the fear of death—have no hold on us now.

Have you ever played tug-of-war? Dozens of people grab a handful of rope and pull in opposite directions—each side trying to overcome the other. For a long time, the tension is strong as each side digs deep. Then, slowly, the balance of power shifts. Once the tide turns it is almost impossible to regain ground. One side overcomes.

Friend, we are in a battle with evil. Our nations, our communities—even our faith communities—are as riddled with unjust systems of greed and power as any in history. It is not enough for us to merely step aside: we must *overcome*. We must advocate for our neighbors, for the strangers and foreigners, even for our enemies. Not with force, hatred, or fear. Not with violence or revenge—but with devotion to each other, with honor, joy, and hospitality, sharing with those in need, rejoicing with those who rejoice, and mourning with those who mourn. With love and goodness. With food and drink.[15] Not as individuals, but together, as a team. As a community.

It sounds naive, doesn't it? A losing battle, a recipe for disaster—at least, if you've seen the unrelentingly violent will of evil. But then again, Jesus was killed for practicing this. Many of his followers were too. Rather than making them fearful, rather than driving them either to silence or violence, Jesus' death and resurrection only solidified their love, their commitment to goodness and overcoming evil through nonviolence.

This is not the wisdom of the world; it is certainly not the American way. But indisputably this *is* Jesus' way, the Christian way. Whether we want to follow Jesus is up to us.

CHAPTER 12

WRESTLING RECONCILIATION

IN THE MIDDLE OF DINNER, my phone rang. I ignored it at first, but when it rang a second time, I picked up and heard my neighbor's anxious voice. We had recently relocated for my husband's job and were neck-deep in an endless stream of expensive relocation complications. The housing market had crashed, and our options for selling our former home ranged from costly to disastrous. Our condo was finally under contract for a short sale at tremendous loss. We were financially intact but worn and tense. This sale felt like the only thing between us and disaster.

My former neighbor Ana[1] skipped the small talk and cut straight to the chase. "I thought you had already moved?" she asked. I assured her we had. "But the sale hasn't gone through yet," she confirmed. Again, I agreed.

"But someone is living in your unit. Did you know that? Did you give them permission?"

No, no we had not.

What felt unbelievable became all too real. Over the next forty-eight hours the story fell into place: A woman had typed up a lease with our address and names, forged our signatures, and signed her own using an alias. She called a locksmith, showed them the lease, and had the locks changed. She called a moving company, who moved her right in.

We were miles away. We didn't see a thing.

Peering into her (our) windows late that night, I could see the formerly empty condo perfectly transformed into a home for someone else. When the police joined us and pounded on the door, she showed them the fraudulent lease. They left.

My husband and I took up vigil at the police department, advocating for action, for justice. We learned far more about criminal, civil, and real-estate law than we cared to know— including these tricky little details: We could not have her charged for breaking and entering or trespassing. We could not change the locks back. We could not legally enter our own property. We could not have her removed. We could not appeal to criminal justice at all. Because she was living in the unit (however illegally), we had no choice but a costly, several-month process of civil-court eviction.

Our closing date on the short sale was just two weeks away. The deal would fall through. Our situation would become untenable.

We were beside ourselves. We hardly slept or went to work. We knocked on the doors of justice without pause. She had committed a crime against us. We were the victims, but the law could do nothing for us. We could not even have a key made to the property, our own home. We experienced a range of emotions we previously did not know existed.

But the more I learned, the more I could not fault the laws themselves, the scales that favored her over me. Thousands of women, often with children, live in men's houses without their own names on the lease, mortgage, or utility bills, sometimes without access to their own money. These women are entirely at the mercy of the far-more resourced and legally powerful men in their lives; should he tire of her and throw them out, where would they go? To protect these women and children, my local laws state that if you so much as keep a toothbrush in a residence, you cannot be forced to leave without the full eviction process.

When this woman moved in, she brought more than a toothbrush. She brought every single household possession she owned—and she brought her children. She had been homeless, so she made them a home in our home. The law—commendably protective of the vulnerable—had rendered me unprotected and without recourse. It could do nothing to help me.

I was locked in a lose-lose battle with a real but invisible enemy. I could not see or speak to her, or her to me. But our lives were spiraling down together.

Then, after a week of holding vigil, on Good Friday the phone rang again: a middle-of-the-night call from the detective. He had broken her alias and discovered criminal charges; the police were on their way to arrest her. We could legally enter our condo. We could not move her things from the house—the sheriff still needed to order this—but the process could be expedited. We could at least change the locks back. We could proceed with the sale.

And so, in the early, early hours of Holy Saturday, we found redemption.

Or did we? Legally, justice had been served. The financial ruin we faced was averted. The law had found a way to restore to us what a criminal had stolen from us.

But as I stood with the detective in the dark, in the condo, I knew the real injustices had not yet even been identified or addressed. I could imagine my former home, the safe place I had brought my babies home from the hospital—but what my eyes showed me was the home she built for *her* babies. I saw their lovies and stuffed animals, their school assignments, their snacks. I saw the stack of televangelist DVDs on her nightstand, along with a prayer book promising financial prosperity for those who pray the right words. I saw the letters she had written and not yet mailed to her ex-husband, the legal papers showing how he had used her and failed her. I saw the stack of interrupted job applications that now would never be mailed. I saw a dozen little icons of hope, of a living woman, of a mother—and a desperate fight for the safety and health of her children. And I saw a broken, traumatized life unfolding for those children, who themselves would soon be asked to make impossible decisions with far too little invested in them. What she did was terrible, illegal; I planned to resist her with every ounce of strength I had. But I could also recognize her Hail Mary attempt at life.

Never before or since have I received such a bittersweet gift: an invitation to look upon an enemy and see her life from the inside out, as intimately and vulnerably as she sees herself.[2]

GOOD GUYS AND BAD GUYS

I suspect that some of God's motivation in asking us to love and forgive our enemies is that it's not always easy to tell the good guys from the bad guys. There's a plank in our own eye, but we only see the speck in everyone else's. Jesus hung out with all sorts of strange folk, but it was the "good," successful, and proper people he confronted the most.

Consider the people Jesus describes in the Beatitudes. What do those people look like today? Jesus promises blessing to those who are poor, who are hungry, who are weeping, who are hated, excluded, and insulted.[3] We're so convinced Jesus is describing us that we don't look to see if the shoe fits. We reinterpret what Jesus said to cast ourselves as the good guys. It can't be the financially or materially poor who receive the Kingdom of God (even though Jesus said so) because that would exclude many of us. He must mean those who *feel* poor in certain ways. He couldn't have meant those who can't afford enough food, as Jesus said, but those who experience a longing for him in their hearts. When in the next breath Jesus pronounces the *Woes* upon those who are rich and well fed, who manage just fine in society—well, he certainly didn't mean *us*—even if I *am* more likely to throw out food gone bad than worry my children are hungry.

Because, honestly, this is the truth: If Jesus were speaking today and declaring someone blessed in that Kingdom, it would be the woman and children who broke into my condo. No discipleship voices anywhere in my life—no mentors, pastors, or trusted Christian friends—asked me to consider things from that angle. She broke the law. Case closed. I'm the good guy, she's the bad guy. Period. My responsibility to her ends when justice under the law is restored—or so I'm told.

But based on Jesus' track record—not to mention the entire Law and Prophets—he would confront *me* and the other Christians in my neighborhood who are well-fed now, who have a place to live, who are comfortable with a society where there is plenty to go around and yet many go without. In the Prophets, God expressed strong feelings about praise and worship offered to him by people who had not first ensured that everyone in the community had access to basic survival and equitable thriving. Yet do we who are comfortable and well-fed and warm do everything we can to care for our community before lifting our voices and hands in worship? No. Not at all. No church usher has ever asked me this question at the door. We don't see this as a necessary part of American life *or* Christian life—even though God commands it again and again and again.

Our insistence on seeing ourselves as the ones Jesus defends—not even considering if we are the ones he challenges—raises questions for me. Are we so afraid of failure that we are unwilling to be confronted by our trustworthy Savior, the Son of God who loves and dies for his enemies, who uses kindness to bring us to repentance, who made himself nothing to be our servant and point us to God? Worse still, is it possible we consider enemies the people Jesus says he will defend? I'm concerned our insecurities, our fear of displeasing God, of failing, of being asked to walk a hard, hard road not only stop us from hearing the loving, challenging voice of God but block us from even seeing the people Jesus wants to bless.

Earlier I pointed out how much we struggle to imagine

God's all-encompassing love for his enemies (who, conveniently, look so much like our own enemies). Like Jonah, we struggle to accept the gift of God's mercy and goodness if it means we don't get to win.

But here is the kicker: God redeeming his enemies is not an affront to us—it is a gift to us. Because

WE ARE THE ENEMIES.

We all are. "While we were God's enemies, we were reconciled to him through the death of his son."[4] There is no difference, no *us* and *them*. We all are the ones to whom God offers food, water, and hospitality; we are the ones God has promised always to care for and never destroy. God loving his enemies is good news . . . for me. For you. For all of us.

When God does draw boundary lines, he does so for different reasons than we do. When God chooses one person, family, or nation, God does so in *order to bless those he did not choose.* When God chose Abram and Sarai, it was so that all peoples on earth would be blessed through them.[5] When God set apart the nation of Israel to be his people, it was God's plan to "make you a light for the Gentiles, that my salvation may reach to the ends of the earth."[6] God's end game is this: "In the last days the mountain of the LORD's temple will be established as the highest of the mountains; it will be exalted above the hills, and all nations will stream to it."[7] Jesus chose disciples not to be the few who would be saved but the ones sent out to serve, to fish for people. The Holy Spirit ignited the church to be a light to the whole world.

When we use our faith to draw enemy lines rather than bless others, we not only miss the point of our mission from God but we invest in the cycles of violence, vengeance, and marginalization we are sent to subvert. Christians cannot be at war with Muslims, even if our government is waging war against Islamic nations; we Christians must serve, welcome, feed, and befriend our Muslim neighbors, strangers, and (if it comes to it) enemies. Christians cannot be at war with folks who prefer to say *Happy Holidays* and don't celebrate Christmas; we Christians must put their rights before our own, prayerfully using whatever social influence we have to seek *their* good. Christians cannot be at war with "liberals" on one side or "fundamentalists" on the other. Our warlike tactics of slander, fearmongering, and "unwholesome talk" are antithetical to the Spirit of Christ. We are empowered to speak our minds in a way that honors others, putting them before ourselves—and, of course, providing hospitality, provision, and care.

TRUTH, RECONCILIATION, FORGIVENESS

Martin Luther King Jr. famously said, "Love is the only force capable of transforming an enemy into a friend."[8] Undoubtably this is true. But taken out of context, it is all too easy for those of us with cultural power or influence to demand forgiveness from those we have wronged without actually changing our damaging behavior. We want forgiveness in the name of love to cover up our sins, without having to repair the damage of our sin. As James H. Cone wrote, "The difficulty is not with the reconciliation-forgiveness question itself but with the people asking it. . . . They who are responsible for the dividing walls of hostility, racism, and hatred want to know whether the victims are ready to forgive and forget—without changing the balance of power."⁹ In other words, it would be *great* if those we harmed—intentionally or unknowingly—chose to love instead of hate us. But this expectation evolves into another form of oppression. We ask others not only to bear the abuse and suffering perpetrated upon them but then to silently extend "grace" and "forgiveness" without experiencing healing and restored dignity. We don't want the powerful perpetrators to feel discomfort.

This common response to sin is an utter misappropriation of love and forgiveness—and the act of loving one's enemies. Reconciliation and restoration require upheaval, truth-telling, and lament.

My family has an enormous garden—which means that, in addition to an enormous harvest, we have an enormous weed problem. I have a special tool that uproots the weeds. A long, narrow strip of metal goes deep, deep underground; I give it just a bit of a nudge and sever the stalks at the root. Then, the entire plant pulls up easily. I go down the rows inch by inch, uprooting one at a time for hours. It would take much less time to simply pull them out by hand. But weeds have not survived in my carefully cultivated bed for nothing: Their strategy is impressive. However small and delicate these plants look above ground, they are thickly and firmly rooted below. I could reconcile my garden quickly, making it look lovely and Instagram-worthy with little effort. But this will not even lightly damage the weeds. By the time the Instagram likes start pouring in, the thick roots will have sent new shoots above ground.

Our real-life sins and evils are just as difficult to uproot.

Surface-level repentance that demands forgiveness without change does nothing to produce reconciliation. When Isaiah talks about God's new creation based on justice and righteousness, he describes the wolf living in harmony with the lamb, the leopard snuggling up to the goat, the calf with the lion, the cow with the bear, a human infant playing in a cobra's nest![10] What is notable is not that the vulnerable in these pairings have learned to forgive; the point is that the predators have utterly and completely changed their ways.[11]

How much upheaval to the natural order would I need to experience before I would place my baby in a cobra's den? In God's justice system, there will be safety for all *only* when the powerful cease to cause harm. That's the level of reconciliation the church is asked to take on.

Shortly after apartheid ended in South Africa in 1994, the Truth and Reconciliation Commission was established to allow both victims and perpetrators of gross human-rights violations to give their statement and tell their story. Thirty-five years of human-rights abuses could not simply be left unaddressed if the country was to transition from oppression to democracy. Real abuse requires real truth-telling. The goal was restorative justice.

Those who were there—and those who listened to the radio and television broadcasts worldwide—recall the voices of men and women wailing, screaming, crying as they spoke the truth of what they had lived through, what they had seen, what had happened to them, and what they had done. There was no hiding from the brutal reality, no sweeping it under the rug or hiding it under a closet. There was no asking the oppressed to be silent lest they hurt the feelings of their oppressors. The country of South Africa—under the leadership of Nelson Mandela and Desmond Tutu, among others—committed to a long, hard look at injustice and the tools of repentance, forgiveness, restoration, and reparation. The love that turns enemies into neighbors[12] does not smooth things over with sweet words of unity but allows the ferocity of suffering to shout itself out, allows lament and restorative justice to do its work. Love requires truth, pain, and confrontation. It requires the powerful "good guys" to publicly reconsider what role they play in the story.

On August 6, 1945, the United States dropped the first atomic bomb on the Japanese city of Hiroshima. Three days later, the USA dropped another bomb, this time on the city of Nagasaki. Over a hundred thousand people were instantly killed when the bombs leveled each city for miles. Another hundred thousand died from injury and radiation sickness in the subsequent weeks and months.[13] As the world faltered under the weight of two entire cities wiped from the planet—nearly all the dead were civilians, families, and children—the United States and her allies celebrated the end of a terrible war and the victory of justice over tyranny.

Koko Kondo was a baby when this bomb fell on her home city, trapping her in the rubble. Her mother dragged her out to relative safety, but the long-term impact on Koko could never be erased. Her childhood was filled with fear and hate, radiation poisoning, and a crystal-clear understanding of the enemy who had stolen everything.

At the very young age of ten years old, Koko had the incredible opportunity to meet the co-pilot of the plane, the American man who dropped the bomb. He told her what he wrote in his log that terrible day: "My God, what have I done." When Koko saw the tears streaming down his face, she thought, *He's the same human being as me. If I hate, I should not hate this guy. I should hate the war itself, which we human beings caused.*[14] In this moment her life's work began: fighting for peace and abolishing nuclear weapons.

In 2018, Rachael Denhollander spoke at the sentencing of Larry Nassar, the former USA Gymnastics doctor. Near the end of her forty-minute talk, she extended forgiveness to the man who had molested her and countless other girls and young women. But her forgiveness did not stand alone. It was surrounded by a compelling speech in which Rachael vividly outlined Nassar's evil acts, calling for the truth to be spoken aloud and for him to receive the fullest penalty possible under the law. These words came after years of costly truth-telling work to indict and convict Nassar.

What Rachael's confrontation made clear is that in Christ, she forgave her enemy. But forgiveness was just the first step; justice against him under the law was still required. Even this form of justice was not enough: The truth must be spoken so resoundingly that restorative justice could begin, that society could start grappling with the larger question of *What is a little girl worth?*[15] Only with each of these in place—truth-telling, forgiveness, legal justice, *and* restorative justice—could the lamb consider approaching the lion. Only then does active, *agapē* love become sincere. With each of these in place, we are positioned to abhor evil and cling to what is good, to overcome evil with good.

GRACE, ALL THE WAY DOWN

We got our condo back on Easter Sunday. My family and I went to church, wrung out and exhausted in a sanctuary decked with lights and colors and ringing with anthems jubilantly declaring the Resurrection—God's redemption unleashed, the firstfruits of a new world, and the full restoration to come.

But my head was spinning.

We had regained legal ownership, but not shalom, not wholeness. I sat in church while she sat in jail. My enemy had sinned against me grievously, and I had the legal right to act against her. But biblical justice and shalom is not about me triumphing over her. True redemption was utterly unreachable—beyond my imagination—from where we both sat. If I have heard Jesus' voice at all, I cannot fully celebrate Easter without this woman. Redemption is restoration of her life *and* mine. Restoration of her life *with* mine.[16]

Nothing about that Easter was abstract for me. Suffering and sin looked me in the face and demanded an answer. Resurrection is useless if it is confined to those of us dressed up nicely on Sunday. I couldn't help but ask: What does Jesus' resurrection mean for *her*, for my enemy in jail, who cried out to God for protection and provision and wound up without even her children?

Jesus did not come to earth and die, breaking down the gates of death and hell, rising again in new life only to restore those so little broken they could run to him, overlooking those so shattered they can neither hear his voice nor lift their arms. It is not restoration if the most broken among us are not made whole. God's redemption must envelop both me and my enemies.

Resurrection reaches all the way down into death and decay and pulls the entire system inside out.

Jesus told his followers to forgive their enemies, then proved he meant it by forgiving the men who killed him even as they crucified him. This is far more than we can do on our own strength. But it is also not nearly enough. Jesus commands not only forgiveness but justice, jubilee, and shalom. Not merely that debts are paid but a society where debts need not be incurred. Together, we must confront the inequalities that create the vulnerable who become our enemies. Because, Jesus said, we are children of God—and God is this way. Because we are citizens of the new creation—and new creation is this way.

So then our mission, should we choose to accept it, is to rewrite the cycle of creating what we fear by overcoming fear. By fearing bravely. By letting our fear of God drive us to a courageous love that casts out fear. Instead of creating fear by our fear, we love what is unlovable and transform it into love.

Even if it costs us dearly.

I never saw this woman or her children, did not ever meet her or speak to her. There is no happy ending to this story—at least, not that I can see, not in this world.

And what of the world to come? I've heard suffering people encourage each other with the assurance that even if their enemies aren't punished in this life, they will be in the next. But her eternal punishment would not result in reconciliation, redemption, or shalom; only in the triumph of evil, the suffering unleashed on the most vulnerable by our unjust world continuing into eternity. This would be the opposite of justice. The opposite of redemption, shalom, wholeness, "made new."

Instead, I believe Jesus invites us to exchange the word *punished* for *peace*. Even if my enemy doesn't find peace in this life, I hope and pray and plead with my Creator that she will find peace in the next.

After all, it was to the poor God promised the Kingdom, those who are weary and sad now, those who are hungry and thirsty now.

Or as writer Laura Jean Truman wrote, "It's grace, all the way down. . . . God's grace is either coming for all of us or none of us—otherwise, we're all just one traumatic childhood away from being cast out of the Presence."[17] Yes, it's grace, all the way down.

THESE THREE REMAIN

Remember the Roman emperor who attempted to rid his land of Christianity, complaining that Christians were serving and loving not only their own but *everyone*—including the people actively trying to eliminate them?[18] That Emperor failed. Christianity has long outlived both that man and the Roman Empire. The Christians did not overcome through fear-fueled war, partisanship, political power moves, or vengeance—but by kindness. By sacrificially loving and providing for anyone they encountered who was in need, and thereby reflecting the image of a loving God, reflecting the image of the world reconciled. Just as God chooses sides to bless those on both sides of the line, we Christ followers bring blessing to those who are for us and those who are against us.

The woman who stole my condo was a stranger who became my enemy, and in so doing made herself my neighbor. To this day, I wrestle with how Jesus would have had me love her.

Looking into the life of my enemy changed me and my understanding of Jesus' words: "From everyone who has been given much, much will be demanded; and from the one who has been entrusted with much, much more will be asked."[19] I'm reminded again why the pronouns in Christianity are plural, not singular: I myself cannot uproot a society's imbalances, not even for one person. But I long to join the team of people who are trying, working for the Kingdom, together overcoming our fears with love, in the power and joy of the Resurrection and the Holy Spirit.

These are costly decisions. We may not be welcomed by our enemies; we may make enemies of our allies. That's why Paul describes us as "hard pressed on every side, but not crushed; perplexed, but not in despair; persecuted, but not abandoned; struck down, but not destroyed."[20]

And so, we forge ahead. Which world will you live for, friend? The kingdom of fear that leads to hate, suspicion, vengeance, and violence disguised as righteousness? Or the Kingdom of the God who first laid down his weapons and then laid down his life, who bears our burdens and carries our sorrows, who places the weary on his shoulders and offers rest?[21]

It will be a hard road. There is no promise of safety or success—at least, not that we will see in this lifetime. We will be sent to unsafe places and unsafe people, and we will be asked to face our fears bravely. But God's Spirit will be with us. Breathe in God's presence, each and every day. Find the community that will empower and support you as you, together, pour your lives out and learn to view your neighbors, strangers, and enemies through a lens of love rather than fear.

Remember that love always protects, always trusts, always hopes, always perseveres. Everything we think we know is fading away, like the dim image in a cloudy glass. But these three remain: faith, hope, and love.

And the greatest of these is love.

BRAVE STEPS

LEARNING TO *ACTUALLY* LOVE AND PRAY FOR OUR ENEMIES—not merely agreeing that Jesus asks it of us—will be the challenge of a lifetime. We will need work, practice, patience, grace, failed attempts, second tries, and the shelter of God's love and the tangible love of others to keep us going. Whether you are reading alone or with a group, these questions, practices, and activities are designed to help you begin the life-long practice of loving and praying for the enemies in your real life and community.

REFLECT AND DISCUSS

What long-term traditions of dislike have you inherited? Reflect on or share the story of how this began and how it came to an end (if it did).

What does God's command to love our enemies teach us about God's character? About ourselves?

In what ways does fear turn *us* into a danger to others? How do we become enemies?

Do you hold views or behaviors that you have considered moral, good, or even godly that may actually be harmful to others? How were these ideas formed, and how can you learn a new way?

Where is there injustice and inequity in your community? How have you directly or indirectly suffered or benefited from this?

If we take Jesus' words seriously, the Kingdom of God is for the poor, hungry, broken, and hopeless. Who is that in your community? How does this differ from how we picture the Kingdom of God?

In what ways have you viewed enemies with fear or hate? How can you begin to view them prayerfully and in love?

PRACTICE

• Spend some time sitting or walking in a place where you feel at peace. As you breathe out, thank God for his forgiveness. As you breathe in, receive his love. Do this as often as you can.

• Practice the Loving-Kindness Meditation. During a time of quiet prayer, imagine yourself surrounded by God's love. Then, bring to mind your loved ones, and widen this space to include them. Then, recall people you don't know well, or have neutral feelings about, and allow the space of God's grace and love to cover them too. Finally, bring to mind enemies, one at a time. Don't begin this process with the person who has harmed you the most; choose instead someone who frustrates or annoys you. Bit by bit, day by day, expand this circle a bit further in your mind. If the process becomes too traumatic, go back to the beginning and rest in God's spacious love. Contact a friend, pastor, spiritual director, or therapist if you need help. Take your time. This is a lifelong practice, not something to complete in one sitting.

- Write down the names of your enemies: people who have harmed or disliked you, or people you have harmed or dislike. This may seem counterproductive, but we cannot heal from brokenness if we won't acknowledge or repent from sins we won't confess. Physically give these names to God, either by lifting them high in the air using your arms and hands, or by laying them on the ground and kneeling at God's feet. Ask God for help and healing. Consider if there are people you need to forgive, or confront, or ask for forgiveness. Don't be hasty, and don't do this alone: Process your convictions with a wise and trustworthy friend who knows you well, or make an appointment with your pastor or therapist. Remember to pray for emotionally or physically dangerous people while maintaining a safe distance.

- Psalm 23 says of God "you prepare a table before me in the presence of my enemies."[22] Set aside fifteen to twenty minutes to sit silently before God and imagine yourself in this verse. Jesus has invited you to this place, invited you to sit at a table full of the abundance of good provision and food and drink. Where are you? What does the table look like? What foods has God prepared for you? What is your posture toward God, and God's posture toward you?

  Now, take a deep breath and ask God to show you someone you view as an enemy. Who is it? What situation or wound do they represent?

Imagine, now, that your enemy is sitting across from you at the table. What do you feel looking across the table at your enemy? Where is Jesus now? What do you find your soul wanting to say to your enemy? To Jesus? Listen. Talk to God about how you feel in this moment. What do you think and see? What do you need? How does God respond?[23]

- Gather a group of friends or your church community to discuss the inequities in your community. If you (like nearly all of us!) are gathering to sing and worship God without ensuring that everyone in your community is provided for and reconciled, repent of this collectively. Ask God how you can pair worshiping God with the justice and reconciliation he has asked us to embody in the world on an ongoing basis. (This will not be a one-night journey!)

- With your Christian community, work to make this reconciliation tangible by taking a first small step to showing love outside your comfort zone. If there is a Jewish congregation in your community, approach the rabbi about having your small group share an interfaith meal. If there is a mosque in your community, do the same, or bring your Muslim neighbors food at sunset during Ramadan to help them break their fast. Research the holidays and celebrations observed in your community and find a simple way to honor that celebration with a gift, presented with a message of welcoming kindness. For example: red-envelope gifts for Chinese New Year, simple jewelry to a quinceañera, or *Pączki* on Fat Tuesday. These attempts can be awkward or miss the mark, but more commonly they are received with appreciation for what they actually are: a welcoming bid for connection.

LOOK AND LISTEN
- *Love Your Enemies* sculpture by Timothy P. Schmalz
- "See the Day" song by Liz Vice

Find this art or music online, then spend some time sitting with it. What do you see and hear? What invitation is God offering you through this?

ACKNOWLEDGMENTS

Don Gates, my agent: Thank you for your ongoing enthusiasm and encouragement. May you always be able to find a grilled-chicken sandwich nearby.

Caitlyn Carlson, my editor: Thank you for *all the things*, especially the text messages and the tater tots. If you couldn't understand my love of karaoke, where would we be? Thank you for editing this book (and me) so bravely.

The NavPress team: Dave Zimmerman, (the aforementioned) Caitlyn Carlson, Elizabeth Schroll, and Olivia Eldridge. Thank you for being incredibly smart and thoughtful, and so much fun to work with. Elizabeth, your copyediting skills are astounding. With you, any book is in good hands. Olivia, thanks for keeping us all on track. Dave, I regret to inform you that I'm still very much alive; so much for book sales! Don Pape, though you've moved on to new adventures, thank you for believing in this book early on.

The Tyndale alliance team: Robin Bermel, Jessica Adams, Whitney Harrison, Linda Schmitt, and Lindsey Bergsma. Wow!

It really does take a village, and I'm grateful for how skilled and supportive you are. Thank you for lending your expertise and artistry to this project. You always make me feel at home.

Aubrey Sampson: I can't image doing this author thing without you. I'm grateful for every Voxer, carpool negotiation, trip to T.J. Maxx, brunch-and-a-movie (I mean, important business meeting), and glass of wine on our porches. Thanks for helping me keep the vampires at bay.

Rosie Delgado: Thank you, thank you, thank you, for being the first to read and offer feedback on the first draft of this manuscript. I hope I have honored your suggestions well; I am grateful for the opportunity to learn from you. The way you serve our community inspires me always.

Melissa Duncan: Thank you for letting me copy your notes and for so many conversations that made my thoughts a little bit clearer. I'm grateful to have a partner on the MDiv journey.

My writing community near and far: Whether we connect on Zoom, Facebook, Twitter, Voxer, or in person, I'm grateful for the ways we go further together. Thank you to the Redbud Writers Guild, the folks at Speaking of Writing, the Writers of Norwich, and all my faithful texting buddies. I would never want to do this without you.

Thank you to my neighbors, who have taught me so much of what this book is about. There are far too many to list here, but a specific thank-you to the Wistrand and Duncan families for braving Messy Mondays with us, and to Joel and Melissa, Saul and Abby for consistently teaching me what it looks like to love strangers and enemies without fear. To the entire Puente del Pueblo community: You have changed my life in all the best ways, and I am forever grateful. Thank you to Jose, Alberta, and Inocencia, Cruz and Victor—as well as so many others—for inviting us to your house for dinner and parties and for letting me learn from your stories. To the families, teachers, staff, board, and administration of D33: You know how much I love and appreciate you. Thank you for the ongoing investments you make in all our children.

To my parents, Gene and Linda: I said a lot of things in this book about my childhood faith, but the two of you have pointed me toward the God of love and away from fear since the very beginning and without wavering. Thank you, thank you, thank you. Thank you.

To my kids, Asher, Benjamin, and Selah: You three are my *magnum opus*. Thank you for being flexible and gracious with me, and for the hugs, treats, and fizzy waters that kept me going. I pray that someday you will read these books and they will make sense to you.

Matthew: Without your partnership, I wouldn't have learned any of this. Thank you for being the orthopraxy to my orthodoxy, an early reader of this manuscript, and my strongest supporter. I'm grateful for your trustworthy counsel and unrelenting enthusiasm . . . not to mention your spaghetti sauces and lattes. Thank you for your strong coparenting skills and for giving me the space and time book writing requires. I love you.

To you, reader: Thank you for picking up this book and wrestling through it with me. I've written all this for you. I pray that we can learn together how to follow Jesus down the path of love that conquers fear.

To you, Jesus: Thank you for inviting us to aim so high and

for your grace that is sufficient to fill in all the gaps. A lifetime of trying, and failing, and trying again is the most beautiful opportunity I can imagine. Thank you for leading us all the way.

LOVE BRAVELY

And now, we step forward, forgetting the fears that are behind us and reaching into the love that is ahead. What will you do with this love as you move toward your neighbors, strangers, and enemies? Share your stories using the hashtag #FearingBravely on Instagram, Facebook, or Twitter.

Connect with Catherine as she beautifully intertwines reality with theology. Don't miss her other books, *Long Days of Small Things: Motherhood as a Spiritual Discipline* and *All Shall Be Well: Awakening to God's Presence in His Messy, Abundant World.*

@catherinemcniel
www.catherinemcniel.com

NOTES

FOREWORD

1. C. S. Lewis, *The Weight of Glory: And Other Addresses* (New York: HarperOne, 2001), 46.

SECTION ONE: DON'T BE AFRAID

1. Luke 24:5-6.
2. Luke 36, 38, 41, slightly paraphrased.

CHAPTER 1: WHOM SHALL I FEAR?

1. Here's an interesting study on a woman who did not experience fear, because of a damaged amygdala: Stephan Hamann, "Affective Neuroscience: Amygdala's Role in Experiencing Fear," *Current Biology* 21, no. 2, https://www.cell.com/current-biology/pdf/S0960-9822 (10)01593-9.pdf.
2. Ralph Adolphs, "The Biology of Fear," *Current Biology* 23, no. 2 (January 2013): R79–R93.
3. Julie Ray, "Americans' Stress, Worry and Anger Intensified in 2018," Gallup, April 25, 2019, https://news.gallup.com/poll/249098/americans -stress-worry-anger-intensified-2018.aspx. Note that this predates the COVID-19 pandemic.
4. "The Complete List of Fears, 2018" from the Chapman University Survey of American Fears Wave 5, accessed June 24, 2021, https:// www.chapman.edu/wilkinson/research-centers/babbie-center/_files/fear -2018/Complete-Fears-2018-ranked.pdf. It's interesting to note that all this research was completed well before the pandemic and other fear-inciting events of 2020.
5. See, for example, (1) Charles Mathewes, "White Christianity Is in Big Trouble. And It's Its Own Biggest Threat," *Washington Post*,

December 19, 2017, https://www.washingtonpost.com/news
/posteverything/wp/2017/12/19/white-christianity-is-in-big-trouble
-and-its-its-own-biggest-threat/; (2) Alex Vandermaas-Peeler et al.,
"Partisan Polarization Dominates Trump Era: Findings from the 2018
American Values Survey," PPRI, October 29, 2018, https://www.prri
.org/research/partisan-polarization-dominates-trump-era-findings
-from-the-2018-american-values-survey/; (3) "A New Survey Suggests
White Evangelicals Are Most Likely to Believe QAnon Conspiracies,"
Relevant, February 11, 2021, https://www.relevantmagazine.com/current
/nation/a-new-survey-suggests-white-evangelicals-are-most-likely-to
-believe-qanon-conspiracies/; and (4) Robert P. Jones, "Racism Among
White Christians Is Higher than Among the Nonreligious. That's No
Coincidence," NBC, July 27, 2020, https://www.nbcnews.com/think
/opinion/racism-among-white-christians-higher-among-nonreligious
-s-no-coincidence-ncna1235045.

6. John 13:35.
7. 1 John 4:18.
8. Hundreds of years before Jesus, a Chinese philosopher wrote in the *Tao Te Ching*, "Through Love, one has no fear." This ancient wisdom— understood by different cultures, religions, and geographies, and central to the way of Jesus—has been confirmed by modern science: When the amygdala overactively churns out fear, what calms and quiets us is oxytocin, sometimes called "the love hormone" or "the bonding hormone."
9. Italicized text is taken from 1 Corinthians 12:31–13:13 and is slightly paraphrased.
10. See Matthew 7:14 and Luke 14:25-33.
11. "The Didache" in *Early Christian Writings: The Apostolic Fathers*, trans. Maxwell Staniforth, ed. Andrew Louth (New York: Penguin Books, 1987), 193.

CHAPTER 2: UNSAFE AND UNAFRAID

1. *Holman Concise Bible Dictionary*, "Cross, Crucifixion" (Nashville: B&H Publishing Group, 2010), 147.
2. Luke 9:23, NLT.
3. Crucifixion was a common weapon of terror employed by the Roman empire. It was not uncommon to round up hundreds of people for a mass crucifixion to spell the threat of revolt and keep the people in line. Josephus writes of two thousand men who were crucified in Galilee in this manner around the time Jesus was born. Imagine growing up in

such conditions: Roman peace was enforced by outrageous terror and violence. "Antiquities of the Jews: Books 17-19," in *The Works of Flavius Josephus*, trans. William Whiston (London: Henry G. Bohn, 1845), 34–35.

4. Matthew 20:22, paraphrased.
5. Huston Smith, *The Soul of Christianity: Restoring the Great Tradition* (San Francisco: HarperSanFrancisco, 2006), 76.
6. "Julian the Apostate, Letters (1923) Works vol. 3, pp. 2-235," trans. W. C. Wright, accessed June 24, 2021, http://www.tertullian.org/fathers /julian_apostate_letters_1_trans.htm.
7. From John 16.
8. This has been historically uncontroversial, though recently many scholars doubt that Paul was the author, suggesting it was penned by one of Paul's disciples, who used Paul's writing as a source or wrote in collaboration with Paul.
9. Ephesian 1:21.
10. Uncontested for decades, per the U.S. News and World Report, power subranking of their annual "Best Countries Ranking," accessed November 6, 2020, https://www.usnews.com/news/best-countries /power-rankings.
11. Romans 6:8.

CHAPTER 3: FEARING GOD
1. Brian Doerksen, "Refiner's Fire" © 1990 by Mercy/Vineyard Publishing.
2. Exodus 20:20.
3. Dr. James Bruckner from North Park Seminary, in his lecture on the Old Testament I attended in spring of 2020; thanks to my classmate Melissa Duncan's note-taking skills for the recall.
4. Romans 12:2, paraphrased. Also see "Oxytocin Helps to Better Overcome Fear," ScienceDaily, November 13, 2014, https://www.sciencedaily.com /releases/2014/11/141113110014.htm.
5. ISV.
6. Mark 8:31-38, emphasis added.
7. While these ideas are touched on in the New Testament, for the most part we read medieval tradition back into the text and find far more there than was said or understood at the time.

SECTION TWO: NEIGHBORS
1. Mark 1:15, paraphrased.
2. Mark 1:17, paraphrased.

CHAPTER 4: NEXT-DOOR STRANGERS
1. Matthew 22:37-40.
2. Leslie Davis and Kim Parker, "A Half-Century after 'Mister Rogers' Debut, 5 Facts about Neighbors in U.S.," Pew Research Center, August 15, 2019, https://pewrsr.ch/2z0sn9h.
3. Though it isn't quoted, I'm grateful to Soong-Chan Rah's work on this in *The Next Evangelicalism: Freeing the Church from Western Cultural Captivity* (Downers Grove, IL: IVP Books, 2009).
4. Gerhard Lohfink, "Did the Early Christians Understand Jesus?: Nonviolence, Love of Neighbor, and Imminent Expectation," *Plough* no. 8, March 30, 2016, https://www.plough.com/en/topics/faith/early -christians/did-the-early-christians-understand-jesus.
5. James 1:1-8.
6. See Romans 12; Corinthians 13; and Galatians 5:13-26.
7. Gerhard Lohfink, "Did the Early Christians Understand Jesus?: Nonviolence, Love of Neighbor, and Imminent Expectation," *Plough* no. 8, March 30, 2016, https://www.plough.com/en/topics/faith/early -christians/did-the-early-christians-understand-jesus.
8. Acts 2:45, 4:37, 5:1.
9. Justin Martyr, "The First Apology," Early Christian Writings, accessed June 24, 2021, http://www.earlychristianwritings.com/text/justinmartyr -firstapology.html.
10. Dionysus, quoted in Gerhard Lohfink, "Did the Early Christians Understand Jesus?: Nonviolence, Love of Neighbor, and Imminent Expectation," *Plough* no. 8, March 30, 2016, https://www.plough .com/en/topics/faith/early-christians/did-the-early-christians -understand-jesus.
11. 1 John 3:17.
12. Matthew 5:13, ISV.
13. Some of this section is roughly taken from a Bible study companion I wrote for *Refuse to Do Nothing* by IVP. Though it does not appear in the published book, it is available for free download from IVP's website: https://www.ivpress.com/Media/Default/Discussion-Guides/4302.pdf.

CHAPTER 5: WHO ARE THE PEOPLE IN YOUR NEIGHBORHOOD?
1. "6. How Urban, Suburban, and Rural Residents Interact with Their Neighbors," from Kim Parker et al., *What Unites and Divides Urban, Suburban, and Rural Communities* (Pew Research Center, May 2018), https://www.pewsocialtrends.org/2018/05/22/how-urban-suburban -and-rural-residents-interact-with-their-neighbors/.

2. This commonly used phrase originated, I believe, with Bryan Stevenson's work. For example: https://www.youtube.com/watch ?v=1RyAwZIHo4Y.
3. Though I don't go into the details in this book, it is worth learning about the legal and policy reasons behind why we live where we live.
4. Jeremiah 29:7.
5. Another problem, as the podcast *Nice White Parents* so well demonstrates, is when privileged parents choose a school in order for their children to benefit from the diversity, yet (unwittingly) turn the resources of the school toward the needs of the powerful and privileged rather than their under-resourced neighbors. This other extreme is also a failure to be a good neighbor.

CHAPTER 6: JUBILEE
1. Luke 12:32.
2. Galatians 5; 1 Corinthians 13.
3. Isaiah 61:1-2, 58:6. The story a paraphrase of Luke 4.
4. Matthew 5:17.
5. Luke 4:16-20.

SECTION THREE: STRANGERS
1. This section is a retelling of Luke 10:25-37.

CHAPTER 7: STRANGER THINGS
1. Gerhard Lohfink, "Did the Early Christians Understand Jesus?: Nonviolence, Love of Neighbor, and Imminent Expectation," *Plough* no. 8, March 30, 2016, https://www.plough.com/en/topics/faith/early -christians/did-the-early-christians-understand-jesus.
2. Betsy Cooper et al., "How Americans View Immigrants, and What They Want from Immigration Reform: Findings from the 2015 American Values Atlas," Public Religion Research Institute, March 2016, https:// www.prri.org/research/poll-immigration-reform-views-on-immigrants/.
3. "Attitudes Toward Refugees Remain Stable Despite Dramatic Changes in U.S. Asylum Policy," Public Religion Research Institute, June 18, 2020, https://www.prri.org/spotlight/attitudes-toward-refugees-remain -stable-despite-dramatic-changes-in-u-s-asylum-policy/.
4. LifeWay Research, *Evangelical Views on Immigration*, February 2015, http://lifewayresearch.com/wp-content/uploads/2015/03/Evangelical -Views-on-Immigration-Report.pdf.
5. Leviticus 19:34, NRSV.

6. Deuteronomy 27:19.
7. Zechariah 7:9-10, NRSV.
8. Ezekiel 47:22, NRSV.
9. Jeremiah 7:5-7, NRSV.
10. 1 John 1:1.
11. Nick Corasaniti, Richard Pérez-Peña, and Lizette Alvarez, "Church Massacre Suspect Held as Charleston Grieves," *New York Times*, June 18, 2015, https://www.nytimes.com/2015/06/19/us/charleston-church -shooting.html.
12. Mark Berman, "'I Forgive You.' Relatives of Charleston Church Shooting Victims Address Dylann Roof," *Washington Post*, June 19, 2015, https://www.washingtonpost.com/news/post-nation/wp/2015 /06/19/i-forgive-you-relatives-of-charleston-church-victims-address- dylann-roof/.

CHAPTER 8: BECOMING ANGELS

1. Romans 12:9, 13, NLT.
2. 1 Peter 4:9, NLT.
3. Hebrews 13:1-2.
4. Christine D. Pohl, *Making Room: Recovering Hospitality as a Christian Tradition* (Grand Rapids, MI: Eerdmans, 1999), xi.
5. For more on this topic, see Pamela Johnston, "'All Strangers and Beggars Are from Zeus': Early Greek Views of Hospitality," *Pacific Journal* 13 (2018): 103–113.
6. Matthew 25:40, paraphrased. For the full account, see Matthew 25:31-26.
7. D. L. Mayfield, *The Myth of the American Dream: Reflections on Affluence, Autonomy, Safety, and Power* (Downers Grove, IL: InterVarsity Press, 2020), 81.
8. Howard Markel and Alexandra Minna Stern, "The Foreignness of Germs: The Persistent Association of Immigrants and Disease in American Society," *Milbank Quarterly*, 80, no. 4 (December 2002): 757–788, https://www.ncbi.nlm.nih.gov/pmc/articles/PMC2690128/.
9. Luke 19:41-42.
10. Matthew 25:14-30.
11. Ezekiel 16:49-50.
12. Luke 10:12. See also Matthew 10:15, 11:24.
13. "Sodom and Gomorrah: A Story about Sin and Judgment," ZA Blog, September 20, 2018, https://zondervanacademic.com/blog/sodom -and-gomorrah.

14. 1 Timothy 3:2.
15. C. S. Lewis, "The Weight of Glory," sermon delivered at University Church of St Mary the Virgin, Oxford, in 1941.
16. "The Didache" in *Early Christian Writings: The Apostolic Fathers*, trans. Maxwell Staniforth, ed. Andrew Louth (New York: Penguin Books, 1987), 196.

CHAPTER 9: THE STRANGE IMAGE OF GOD

1. Justo L. González, *The Story of Christianity, Volume 1: The Early Church to the Dawn of the Reformation*, rev. and updated (New York: HarperOne, 2010), 149–168.
2. Laurie A. Rudman and Kris Mescher, "Of Animals and Objects: Men's Implicit Dehumanization of Women and Likelihood of Sexual Aggression," *Personality and Social Psychology Bulletin* 38, no. 6 (June 2012): 734–46, https://journals.sagepub.com/doi/full/10.1177/0146167212436401.
3. Nour Kteily et al., "The Ascent of Man: Theoretical and Empirical Evidence for Blatant Dehumanization," *Journal of Personality and Social Psychology* 109, no. 5, 901–31,https://doi.apa.org/doiLanding?doi-10.1037%2Fpspp0000048.
4. Allison Skinner, "The Slippery Slope of Dehumanizing Language," The Conversation, June 4, 2018, https://theconversation.com/the-slippery-slope-of-dehumanizing-language-97512.
5. 1 Corinthians 13:6.
6. Rajesh Thind (@RajeshThind), Twitter, September 9, 2019, 6:32 a.m., https://twitter.com/RajeshThind/status/1171038619378864129.
7. 2 Timothy 2:23, ESV.
8. Matthew 9:10-17; Mark 2:15-22; Luke 5:29-39.
9. 1 Corinthians 1:27.
10. As quoted in Gordon D. Fee, New International Commentary on the New Testament: *The First Epistle to the Corinthians*, (Grand Rapids, MI: Eerdmans, 1987), 81.
11. Michael J. Kruger, "How Early Christianity Was Mocked for Welcoming Women," *Canon Fodder* (blog), July 13, 2020, https://www.michaeljkruger.com/how-early-christianity-was-mocked-for-welcoming-women/?fbclid=IwAR0SO2NO-5Ogka8vx0BmYZGeX4zOGNM2sDQEWNjHV2O2erKbYQL0L_OXTD4.
12. Melissa Florer-Bixler, *Fire by Night: Finding God in the Pages of the Old Testament* (Harrisonburg, VA; Herald Press, 2019), 145.
13. Florer-Bixler, *Fire by Night*, 146.

SECTION THREE BRAVE STEPS

1. Hodler painted this event twice (in 1875 and again in 1886); both paintings are titled "The Good Samaritan." I am referencing the one from 1875.

SECTION 4: ENEMIES

1. See Acts 9 for the full account. Some of the dialogue in this section is paraphrased.

CHAPTER 10: A HARD TEACHING

1. I learned of Daniel's story here: Jared Diamond, "Vengeance Is Ours," *New Yorker*, April 14, 2008, https://www.newyorker.com/magazine /2008/04/21/vengeance-is-ours.
2. Matthew 5:43-44.
3. Adapted from The Jesus Prayer, https://www.orthodoxprayer.org/Jesus %20Prayer.html.
4. Leviticus 19:18.
5. Matthew 5:45.
6. Luke 6:27-36.
7. Blue Letter Bible, "Lexicon: Strong's G2190—*echthros*," accessed June 24, 2021, https://www.blueletterbible.org/lang/lexicon/lexicon.cfm ?Strongs=G2190&t=NIV.
8. I first learned the difference between these two words in this sermon: Todd Hunter, "Love Your Enemies, Really?" Church of the Savior, November 2, 2019, https://friendsofthesavior.org/sermons/love-your -enemies-really-bishop-todd-hunter.
9. Blue Letter Bible, "Lexicon: Strong's G25—*agapaō*," accessed June 24, 2021, https://www.blueletterbible.org/lang/lexicon/lexicon.cfm?Strongs =G25&t=NIV.
10. Flavius Josephus, *The Antiquities of the Jews*, book 17, chap. 10, https:// www.gutenberg.org/files/2848/2848-h/2848-h.htm#link172HCH0010.
11. I owe Scot McKnight, *The Story of God Bible Commentary: Sermon on the Mount* (Grand Rapids, MI: Zondervan, 2013), 143, for these thoughts.
12. John 8:2; Romans 12:2.

CHAPTER 11: OUR NONVIOLENT GOD

1. This song seems to be called "God Loves a Cheerful Giver." I was unable to locate a full citation.
2. Genesis 5:29, ESV.
3. Genesis 6:12.

4. Genesis 8:21.
5. Some of this section was formerly on my blog; http://catherinemcniel
.com/blog/noahs-flood-god-changes-his-mind/. My thoughts on Noah's
story were informed by Walter Brueggemann in *Genesis: Interpretation: A
Bible Commentary for Teaching and Preaching* (Atlanta: John Knox Press,
1982) and *An Introduction to the Old Testament: The Canon and Christian
Imagination* (Louisville, KY: Westminster John Knox Press, 2003).
6. See, for example, Deuteronomy 7:9-10; Nehemiah 9:17; Psalm 86:4-5,
15; and Joel 2:12-14 (to name just a few).
7. Isaiah 53:7, ESV.
8. Slight paraphrase of John 1:14, MSG.
9. Matthew 5:38-42.
10. Luke 6:36.
11. Gerhard Lohfink, "Did the Early Christians Understand Jesus?:
Nonviolence, Love of Neighbor, and Imminent Expectation," *Plough*
no. 8, March 30, 2016, https://www.plough.com/en/topics/faith/early
-christians/did-the-early-christians-understand-jesus.
12. Isaiah 2:3-4—"Come, let us go up to the mountain of the LORD, to the
temple of the God of Jacob. He will teach us his ways, so that we may
walk in his paths." The law will go out from Zion, the word of the Lord
from Jerusalem. He will judge between the nations and will settle disputes
for many peoples. They will beat their swords into plowshares and their
spears into pruning hooks. Nation will not take up sword against nation,
nor will they train for war anymore.
13. Martin Luther King Jr., "Letter from Birmingham Jail," 1963, though I
found this quote in *True to Our Native Land: An African American New
Testament Commentary* (Minneapolis: Fortress Press, 2007), 269.
14. From Romans 12:9-21.
15. From Romans 12:9-21.

CHAPTER 12: WRESTLING RECONCILIATION
1. Certain details in this story have been intentionally changed or obscured.
2. Thank you to Paraclete Press for permission to use some of the
thoughts and writing from my earlier piece, "Passover, Betrayal, and
Deep Redemption" in *Everbloom: Stories of Living Deeply Rooted and
Transformed Lives* (Brewster, MA: Paraclete Press, 2017), 147–155.
3. Luke 6:20-26.
4. Romans 5:10.
5. Genesis 12:3.
6. Isaiah 49:6.

7. Isaiah 2:2.
8. Martin Luther King Program, "Famous Quotes on Nonviolence," Washington State University, accessed June 25, 2021, https://mlk.wsu.edu/about-dr-king/famous-quotes/.
9. James H. Cone, *God of the Oppressed*, rev. ed. (Maryknoll, NY: Orbis Books, 1997), 207.
10. Isaiah 11.
11. Thanks to Melissa Duncan for the conversation about Jesus, justice, and Isaiah that sparked the thoughts in this paragraph.
12. I don't want to overstate the success of this commission. It was a powerful first step, but there is still much ground that must be covered before these former enemies are truly neighbors—literally and figuratively.
13. "Bombing of Hiroshima and Nagasaki," History.com, updated April 26, 2021, https://www.history.com/topics/world-war-ii/bombing-of-hiroshima-and-nagasaki.
14. Lulu Garcia-Navarro, "An Atomic Bomb Survivor on Her Journey from Revenge to Peace," NPR, August 9, 2020, https://www.npr.org/2020/08/09/900553387/an-atomic-bomb-survivor-on-her-journey-from-revenge-to-peace.
15. Rachael asks this in her victim impact statement, which can be read here: https://www.cnn.com/2018/01/24/us/rachael-denhollander-full-statement/index.html. It became the title of her 2019 book with Tyndale: *What Is a Girl Worth?: My Story of Breaking the Silence and Exposing the Truth about Larry Nassar and USA Gymnastics*.
16. Again, thank you to Paraclete Press for permission to use some of the thoughts and writing from my earlier piece, "Passover, Betrayal, and Deep Redemption" in *Everbloom*, 147–155.
17. Laura Jean Truman, "Hell, No: Why Grace Is Coming for Us All," blog, October 17, 2020, https://laurajeantruman.com/2020/10/17/hell-no-why-grace-is-coming-for-us-all/.
18. Julian the Apostate, in his letter to Arsacius; available here: http://www2.latech.edu/~bmagee/201/swinburn/Julian.html.
19. Luke 12:48.
20. 2 Corinthians 4:8-9.
21. Matthew 11:28.
22. Psalm 23:5.
23. Thank you to Rob Peterson, DMin, spiritual director and faculty at North Park Theological Seminary, for walking me through this exercise and allowing me to share it.

THE NAVIGATORS® STORY

———— ☽ ————

T HANK YOU for picking up this NavPress book! We hope it has
been a blessing to you.

NavPress is a ministry of The Navigators. The Navigators began
in the 1930s, when a young California lumberyard worker named
Dawson Trotman was impacted by basic discipleship principles and
felt called to teach those principles to others. He saw this mission as
an echo of 2 Timothy 2:2: "And the things you have heard me say in
the presence of many witnesses entrust to reliable people who will
also be qualified to teach others" (NIV).

In 1933, Trotman and his friends began discipling members of the
US Navy. By the end of World War II, thousands of men on ships and
bases around the world were learning the principles of spiritual multi-
plication by the intentional, person-to-person teaching of God's Word.

After World War II, The Navigators expanded its relational ministry
to include college campuses; local churches; the Glen Eyrie Conference
Center and Eagle Lake Camps in Colorado Springs, Colorado; and neighborhood and citywide initiatives across the country and around the world.

Today, with more than 2,600 US staff members—and local ministries in more than 100 countries—The Navigators continues the transformational process of making disciples who make more disciples, advancing the Kingdom of God in a world that desperately needs the hope and salvation of Jesus Christ and the encouragement to grow deeper in relationship with Him.

NAVPRESS was created in 1975 to advance the calling of The Navigators by bringing biblically rooted and culturally relevant products to people who want to know and love Christ more deeply. In January 2014, NavPress entered an alliance with Tyndale House Publishers to strengthen and better position our rich content for the future. Through *The Message* Bible and other resources, NavPress seeks to bring positive spiritual movement to people's lives.

If you're interested in learning more or becoming involved with The Navigators, go to navigators.org. For more discipleship content from The Navigators and NavPress authors, visit thedisciplemaker.org. May God bless you in your walk with Him!

navpress.com

CP1308